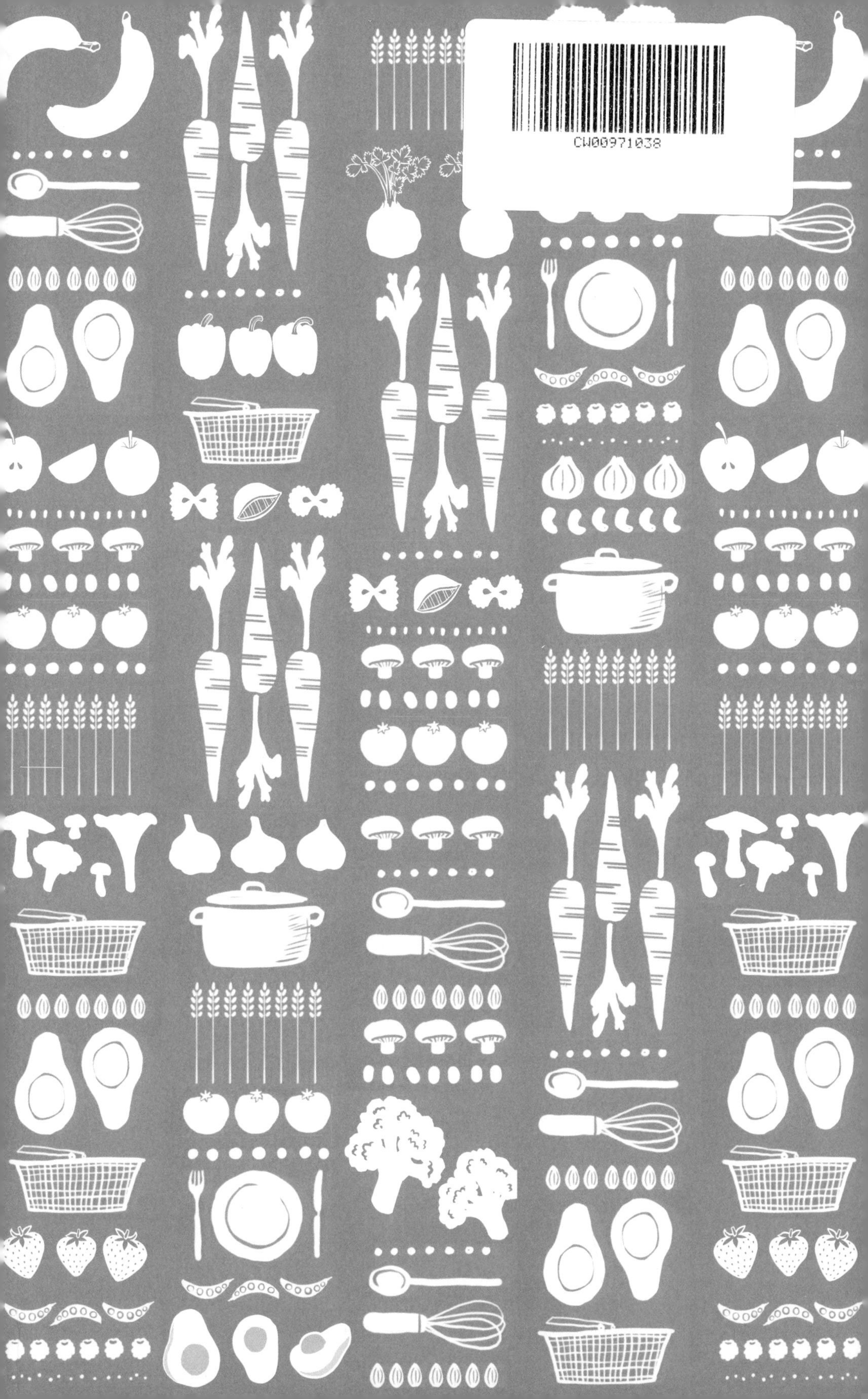
CW00971038

EAT TO SAVE THE PLANET

ANNIE BELL

EAT TO SAVE THE PLANET

Over 100 recipes and ideas for eco-friendly cooking and eating

First published 2020 by One Boat
an imprint of Pan Macmillan
6 Briset St, Farringdon, London EC1M 5NR
Associated companies throughout the world
www.panmacmillan.com

ISBN 978-1-5290-47592

9 8 7 6 5 4 3 2 1
A CIP catalogue record for this book is available from the British Library.

Printed and bound in Italy

CONTENTS

Introduction **12**

The environment **21**

Waste not, want not **24**

Grainology **47**

One egg dishes **59**

Comforting stews and curries **85**

All-in-one roasts and pies **113**

Beyond potatoes **147**

Frying pan suppers **165**

Pasta and pilafs **193**

Planetary Health Diet challenge **213**

Meal plan **220**

Appendix A: Planetary Health Diet scientific targets **238**

Appendix B: Before and after Covid-19 **243**

About the author **245**

Acknowledgements **246**

Index **247**

INDEX OF RECIPES

WASTE NOT, WANT NOT

Riches from the rubble soup **40**

Vegetable stock **41**

Veggie mash **42**

Tomato and bread salad **42**

Born-again bread **43**

Herb purée **43**

Breakfast smoothies **44**

Roasted seeds **45**

Banana pancakes with maple syrup **46**

ONE EGG DISHES

Pissaladière omelette **62**

Spinach and scamorza pizza omelette **64**

Leek and Emmental scrambled eggs **66**

Egg-fried spelt **67**

Ranchos eggs with cauliflower and lentils **68**

Griddled broccoli and poached eggs with pine nut breadcrumbs **69**

Salmon salad Niçoise **70**
Corn tortillas with broad bean guacamole and fried eggs **71**
Deep-filled mushroom omelette **72**
Halloumi pittas with poached eggs **73**
Toasted goat's cheese with garlic spinach **74**
Simply pancakes **75**
Breakfast pancakes **76**
Supper pancakes **77**
Spinach and Parmesan pancakes **78**
Spicy omelette strips **79**
Poached and fried eggs **81**

COMFORTING STEWS AND CURRIES

Lamb, date and tomato tagine **88**
Thai chicken and edamame bean curry **89**
Healthy planet chilli con carne **91**
Vegan chilli **92**
Beef hotpot with olives and pickled lemon **94**
Chicken and broad bean stew with pomegranate **95**
Spicy Lebanese lamb stew **97**
Green vegetable minestrone with mint and almond pesto **98**
Red pepper confit **99**
Lamb and butternut stew with pine nuts **100**
Chilli prawn and chickpea stew **102**
Simply salmon and pea fish stew **103**
Slow-roasted tomato sauce and roast tomatoes **104**

Herby seafood stew 105
Scallop tikka 106
Coconut dal curry 107
Pan-fried mackerel 108
Garlicky white beans with spinach 110

ALL-IN-ONE ROASTS AND PIES

Healthy planet lasagne 116
Tomato and basil lasagne 118
Crispy-topped shepherd's pie 120
Cassoulet with walnut crumbs 122
Spinach, nut and goat's cheese pie 123
Root veg and apple pie 124
Chicken and mushroom pie with cauliflower mash 125
Chilli beef pie with aubergine 127
Fish pie with pecan crumble 129
Irish stew pie 130
Roast chicken and roots with persillade 132
Crispy chicken thighs with fiery chickpea dip 134
Roast Romanesco and spring onion salad with balsamic dressing 135
Spicy cauli with turmeric yoghurt 136
Chicken with spinach and padrón peppers 137
Rack of lamb with pesto potatoes 140
Roast beetroot and asparagus roast 142
Roast celeriac, carrot and apple 144
Miso-glazed courgette and peppers 145

BEYOND POTATOES

Bulgur wheat pilaf **150**

Cocktail nut pilaf **151**

Lemon and pine nut brown rice pilaf **152**

Haricot bean smash **154**

Cannellini bean mash with roast peppers **155**

Beetroot mash with wild mushrooms **156**

Pea and mint mash **157**

Broccoli mash with sesame seeds **158**

Honey and sesame roast roots **159**

Roast cabbage with almonds **160**

Courgette chips **161**

Celeriac wedges **162**

Straw celeriac cake **163**

FRYING PAN SUPPERS

Healthy planet burgers **168**

Vegan burgers **169**

Paprika chicken with pecan and coriander salsa **171**

Minty lamb steaks with anchovy rainbow chard **172**

Aubergine-wrapped Greek sausages with roast tomatoes **174**

Quinoa and sugar snap stir-fry **176**

Healthy planet steak and mash **177**

Vegan 'steaks' **178**

Sesame mackerel with orange and beetroot salad **180**

Mackerel with walnut dressing **182**
Seared tuna with cucumber and edamame salsa **183**
Crispy salmon with freekeh and cavolo **185**
Seabass fish fingers with tartare sauce **188**
Salmon with spinach and chickpeas **190**

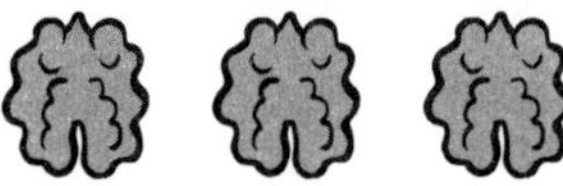

PASTA AND PILAFS

Lamb pilaf with watermelon-and-lemon relish **196**
Asparagus speltotto with crab **198**
Speedy cauliflower, lentil and watercress risotto **199**
Spinach and millet porridge with cashews **200**
Bulgur wheat, cashew nut and rocket pilaf **202**
Tomato and chicken spelt with basil and pistachio pesto **203**
Salmon and spinach with red lentil fusilli **205**
Courgette and goat's cheese with chickpea penne **206**
Roast chicken and mushrooms with spelt casarecce **207**
No-cook crab and buckwheat spaghetti **209**
Black bean spaghetti with sausage and peppers **210**
Watercress and asparagus with green pea penne **211**

PLANETARY HEALTH DIET CHALLENGE

Avo nut butter **228**

Figgy granola **229**

Whole oat porridge **230**

Multi-grain porridge **230**

Bircher muesli **232**

Cheese oatcakes **233**

Sticky granola balls **234**

Nut butter dressing **235**

Silken tofu with sesame **236**

INTRODUCTION

I am old enough to remember winters that were cold. It was the 1960s. Stepping out of the house and exhaling a cloud of steam, the line of foil-topped milk bottles on the step, pecked open by blue tits short of food. Treading carefully on the silvery film of ice on the tarmacked drive to avoid slipping, and the ritual scraping down of the windscreen while the car belched its exhaust into the air. Drawing pictures on the condensation on the windows as my mother furiously tried to de-steam the windscreen with the back of her glove. These were all a normal part of a winter's morning on the way to school.

This year, as we near spring, I have scraped the windscreen down just once. Thick coats, mufflers and hats gather dust in the wardrobe. And as I write, in January, a climbing rose that is usually in bloom from June onwards is flowering in front of a backdrop of mimosa, a hardy blossom prepared to brave snow – not something it has had to do for some years now.

Such anecdotes are of course observational and unscientific, except that recent science does support the perception that winter is no longer winter as I knew it in the 1960s. Instead it is a long, drizzly drawl of a season that lies halfway between autumn and spring, with no real identity to it other than the increased frequency of storms and flooding that have become the norm.

Looking beyond my own back yard, and the small observations that mark personal experience, how could I not be seized with fear and sadness by apocalyptic wild fires raging in Australia, the Amazon, Siberia and Europe, alarmed by the extreme weather, the record temperatures, or the penguins and polar bears displaced from their natural habitats by melting ice caps? I have to pinch myself to believe that they are real. If there is any comfort, it is knowing that I am far from helpless. I can live the changes that will help to eradicate such events. I may be one minuscule part of the whole, but I can still play my part, in particular through the choices I make about how I eat.

A GLIMMER OF HOPE

The million-dollar question is 'how?'. 'How can I eat in a way that is healthy, and good for the planet? How do I know what to believe or how to achieve it?' For years we have been bombarded with advice to increase our fruit and veg intake, lower salt, replace saturated fats with unsaturated, give croissants and white bread a wide berth. All well and good. But layered on top of that, which of us hasn't stood hesitantly in front of a display of produce, wondering about the environmental impact of our food choices? Should we buy organic or conventional, does it involve genetic modification (GM), is it better to buy local or to provide support to developing countries through trader schemes? Are brown paper bags more sustainable than biodegradable ones? It's hardly surprising that eating has become a source of anxiety and that so many are driven to some type of orthorexia in the belief they are solving at least some of these problems.

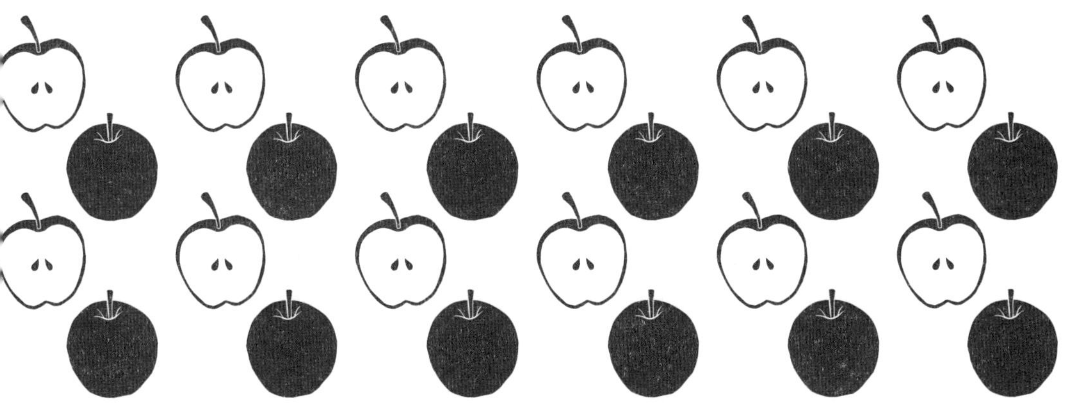

When I first encountered the Planetary Health Diet – recommended in the rather grandly titled report 'Food in the Anthropocene'[1] – it was like a weight lifting off my shoulders. I thought 'at last'. Finally someone has come up with a solution that ticks all of these boxes. Here was a 'diet' – or rather a way of eating – designed to save the world, which simply recommended how much of each food group we should eat. Nothing more and nothing less. It doesn't matter what your dietary persuasion is, whether you are vegan, vegetarian, pescatarian or flexitarian, or, for that matter, where you are in the world. It is ultimately adaptable and as relevant if you are in Tokyo as it is if you live in New York, London or Berlin. It is so simple, it makes you wish someone had come up with it sooner.

Why haven't they? Well, when you look at the scope of the report, it becomes obvious the extent to which the authors have achieved the impossible. The report involved a group of scientists gathered from around the world to create the EAT–*Lancet* Commission, which comprised 19 Commissioners and 18 co-authors from 16 countries. They were asked a very simple question: 'Is it possible to feed a global population of nearly 10 billion people a healthy diet, sustainably, by 2050?'. The answer that came back was 'yes'. Addressing every aspect of our food chain, from farming to nutrition, the results are encapsulated in this extraordinary pared-back way of eating.

However, there are always 'buts' with these things, and no less with this. And the big 'but' here is that for the world to take this way of eating on board, it will require a massive food transformation, one in which politicians and policy makers, farmers and consumers come together. As consumers our role is twofold: the starting point is what we eat, and, following through from that, making the most of what we buy or grow by reducing our food loss and waste.

EATING TO SAVE THE PLANET

The Planetary Health Diet couldn't be more timely. Here is a diet that goes way beyond good nutrition, that treats our health and the environment as a common agenda. It tells us how we should eat not only to maximize our own good health, but also to halt the steady degradation of the planet at the same time.

It is estimated there are over 820 million people around the world who don't have enough food to eat.[2] You can double that figure if you also include those people whose diet is lacking in essential micronutrients (vitamins and minerals). And as a result of this, incidences of obesity and diseases such as coronary heart disease, stroke and diabetes, are all on the up. This fact also links to the Covid-19 pandemic, as all of these were underlying risk factors in terms of the severity of the virus.[3] There are more reasons than ever before why we need to address the unhealthy diets that today present this massive burden of disease globally.

THERE ARE OVER 820 MILLION PEOPLE AROUND THE WORLD WHO DON'T HAVE ENOUGH FOOD TO EAT

Lack of nourishment, be it under-nutrition, over-nutrition or malnutrition, cannot be separated from the environment when so many of the earth's systems have been pushed to their limits. The danger of the world continuing to eat in this way is that we will fail to meet the UN Sustainable Development Goals (SDGs)[4] and the Paris Agreement.[5] And as the planet becomes degraded, this will lead to more malnutrition and the diseases that follow on from that. It becomes a self-perpetuating cycle.

The Planetary Health Diet offers to interrupt that circuit. For the first time ever, a way of eating is being proposed that is based on a set of globally agreed scientific targets that will protect the environment (see page 238). To date, one of the greatest barriers to protecting the environment has been a lack of cohesion. Equally so nutrition, when every country has a different set of standards. So this coming together with common goals is potentially an incredibly powerful tool in achieving real change around the world.

In a nutshell, the diet addresses nutrition globally, at the same time as ensuring that the UN Sustainable Development Goals (SDGs) and the Paris Agreement are achieved. So these are breathtakingly ambitious goals that have never before been attempted. But, finally, we have a blueprint for what we should eat, not only for ourselves, but also for generations to come, by safeguarding food supplies.

HOW TO EAT

Now to the great unveiling: 'What can we eat?' The bedrock of our diet will be plant foods – whole grains, legumes, nuts, vegetables and fruit. From here it closely tracks the Mediterranean diet, which has long been regarded as the gold standard in nutrition. This means using unsaturated oils, such as extra virgin olive oil, rather than animal fats. The diet includes just a small amount of animal protein, with the emphasis on fish and poultry, and red meat as an occasional treat. Equally, the diet can be adapted to suit vegans and vegetarians (see *Vegan, Vegetarian, Pescatarian or Flexitarian?* on page 18).

The recommendations per day break down as follows:

Eggs	13g
Fish	28 g
Meat	14g
Poultry	29g
Dairy:	
Whole milk	250ml
Natural yoghurt	250g
Low-fat cheese (ricotta, mozzarella)	45g
High-fat cheese (Emmental, Cheddar, Parmesan)	30g
Butter	10g
Nuts	50g
Beans, lentils, etc. (dry)	75g
Grains (dry)	232g
Starchy vegetables	50g
Vegetables	300g
Fruit	200g
Added fats[6]	
Unsaturated oils	40g
Saturated oils	11.8g
Added sugar	31g

Energy requirements

The Planetary Health Diet is based on an intake of 2,500 kcal per day, the average energy needs for a man weighing 70kg aged 30 years, and a woman weighing 60kg aged 30 years, with a moderate to high level of physical activity.

But what do the diet's recommendations per day look like in practice? What kind of food does this amount to, and what does the average day hold in store on the plate? These are the questions I wanted answered as I started writing this book. The ideal for any of us is for this way of eating to become second nature, and for that to happen, we need to explore how we can eat.

GREAT FOOD TRANSFORMATION

The big attraction of the Planetary Health Diet is for flexitarians (of which I am one). It is ideal for those who have already signed up to eat more plant foods, who cannot imagine life without enjoying meat, fish and poultry, but who want to do so in a way that is healthy and also supports the planet. It is a 'win-win' diet.

Keeping it simple, our targets for major protein sources come down to about one serving of dairy foods per day, and one serving of other animal-sourced protein per day (so by accruing our daily recommended doses, we can have a serving of chicken twice a week, fish twice a week, eggs and red meat once a week). But the quantities of these food types are still much smaller than we are used to. Whereas usually I might allow 150–200g of meat, fish or poultry per portion, we now have 100g or less to work with.

It is easy to see how many of our favourite traditional dishes are immediately out of bounds. Roasts, steaks, burgers, chops and fillets are immediately challenged by the 100g at a sitting. We are used to hearing the mantra 'better quality, less often', but even that fails to marry with the quantities being mooted. And what about eggs? One and a half a week? Where does this leave our beloved breakfast fry-up, not to mention the occasional frittata or omelette. Back to the drawing board.

In the recipes that follow, meat, fish and poultry are to be savoured as a treat, a luxury to be spun out with other ingredients. There are many cultures around the world that have a tradition of dishes that make good use of small quantities of animal protein. I have also redesigned some of our favourite traditions – the roasts, pies and burgers that we so love – by combining small quantities of meat, fish and poultry with plant-food sources. For some key favourites, such as burgers or lasagne, you will find a Healthy Planet recipe with a vegetarian or vegan option, too. As for eggs, it is amazing just how many lovely dishes you can cook with a single egg once you start adding in plant foods, as the One egg dishes chapter (see page 59) sets out to illustrate.

Many of the recipes are enriched with a substantial inclusion of whole grains, the ascendant ancient grains such as spelt and millet, and the pseudo-cereals like quinoa and buckwheat. These are explored in greater detail in the chapter Grainology (see page 47), given how central they are to this way of eating. The rather meagre recommendation for starchy vegetables is another area to be addressed, so the chapter Beyond potatoes (see page 147) has lots of ideas for side dishes that will stand in for the usual potato mash, roast or chips.

VEGAN, VEGETARIAN, PESCATARIAN OR FLEXITARIAN?

The Planetary Health Diet is designed to cater to all four tribes. But with so much flexibility, the question remains: is there a preferable dietary pattern? Is it better to be vegan or flexitarian if we want to protect the planet?

The diet, which was modelled on all four dietary patterns, took diet and health as the starting point, without any prejudgements about whether one way of eating was preferable to another. A vegan diet, however, is lacking in vitamin B12 as well as running low in other nutrients, and it scored lower than other ways of eating. In particular, being a pescatarian was found to be marginally more beneficial.

On the environmental side, there are arguments for and against whether to include animal protein in your diet or not. A vegan diet means less greenhouse gases, but in terms of the number of people that can be fed there is a disadvantage, considering that grazing is one of the few uses for land in some areas.

Many cultures are compatible with flexitarian diets, for example the traditional Mediterranean diet. So the conclusion is that yes, if you prefer to be vegan that is fine, but we can also continue to eat animal proteins with a clear conscience in the quantities recommended, though for most of us this will involve eating more plant foods than we do at the moment.

PLANT FOOD QUALITY

Reducing how much animal protein we eat is a golden opportunity to bolster our nutrition with plant foods. Plant proteins can be found in all of the major plant food groups, that is legumes, whole grains, nuts and vegetables, in varying quantities. Nuts and legumes are renowned for being rich protein sources, but grains, too, contain a decent amount, and some vegetables such as broccoli, cauliflower, asparagus and sweetcorn are surprisingly good sources.

When it comes to animal or plant protein in relation to nutrition, the scales are finely balanced. On the one hand, animal proteins boast all nine essential amino acids (that is those that the body either can't make or can't make in sufficient quantity), with a high bio-availability: 90–99 per cent will be utilized compared to only 70–90 per cent of a plant protein. Animal proteins also contain vitamin B12, which vegans will need to supplement, and iron too can be lacking in a vegan diet. But, in their favour, plant proteins are lower in saturated fat and contain lots of beneficial micronutrients, as well as fibre, phytochemicals and complex carbohydrates.

The main point with plant proteins is not to fret too much over individual sources and what or how much they contain, or which amino acids; eating across the spectrum is the way to go.

TAKING THE DIET TO THE NEXT LEVEL

The big shift is to move towards a plant-based diet, whether that is as a flexitarian, pescatarian, vegetarian or vegan. But there will be good and bad ways of producing food, and one way that we can take the diet to the next level as consumers is to seek out accreditation schemes or certification. They should be transparent and clear and there to support the environment and our health, be it to do with how plant foods have been grown, or welfare standards for meat, poultry and fish. Such schemes can stand as a set of minimal standards that are otherwise hard to ascertain when we are shopping.

I recommend that you always buy free-range eggs and poultry, and look out for high-welfare certification schemes for your meat – these will differ from region to region. Ensure that fish and shellfish is sustainable, whether wild caught or farmed, and check it's supported by marine conservation schemes, such as the Marine Stewardship Council (MSC), or other ecological certification.

THE ENVIRONMENT

UNHEALTHY BODIES, UNHEALTHY PLANET = LOSE-LOSE DIET

The changes that have taken place in the way we eat over the last fifty years makes the food from my childhood seem unrecognizable. A lot of that change has been for the good. Certainly, increases in crop yields and changes to production practices have led to less hunger, life expectancy has risen globally, and infant and child mortality has fallen. But the flip side is the insipid shift to unhealthier diets that are high in calories and low in nutrition. All the shelves of ultra-processed foods and fast junk-food outlets amount to cheap, empty energy, which has led to a rise in obesity and diseases such as Type 2 diabetes, heart disease and cancer.

Whereas in Victorian times malnutrition meant starvation, today there is an apparent contradiction, as undernutrition sits side by side with obesity, sometimes within the same family. At the same time, the environment is being increasingly degraded.

When you consider that food production is the greatest driver of global environmental change, our power as consumers to protect the planet becomes apparent. Some 40 per cent of land globally is taken up with agriculture, and food production accounts for up to 30 per cent of greenhouse-gas emissions and 70 per cent of freshwater use. And then there is land-system change, when land is converted to farmland, and species are threatened with extinction. The overuse

IMPACT OF FOOD PRODUCTION ON GLOBE

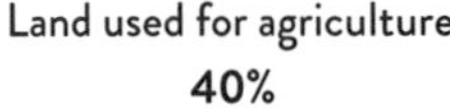

Greenhouse gas emissions
30%

Freshwater use
70%

and misuse of nitrogen and phosphorus fertilizers creates dead zones in lakes and in coastal waters. Meanwhile, some 60 per cent of fish stocks globally are now fully fished, 30 per cent overfished, and catch has been declining since the end of the last century. Add to this that fish farming can negatively affect coastal water as well as freshwater and the land in the vicinity. When you put this devastating environmental cost together with unhealthy dietary patterns, it amounts to a lose-lose diet. We lose and so does the planet.

HEALTHY BODIES, HEALTHY PLANET = WIN-WIN DIET

One way many of us approach eating for the environment is to choose a production system, organic for instance, that we believe best supports the land. Or, we make value judgements about particular crops being good or bad for the environment. But such judgements applied to the wider world would inevitably limit solutions. As Professor Walter Willett, the co-chair of the 'Food in the Anthropocene' report, says, it's not an argument about whether avocados or almonds are good or bad, or organic versus conventional farming, 'it's the right crop, in the right place, produced in the right way that is important'.[7] What is right for one particular region and situation may not be sustainable in another. So there is no single answer for every place in the world.

In the interests of flexibility, instead of being overly prescriptive, the group of international scientists who made up the EAT-*Lancet*

Commission (see page 14) devised a set of global targets. These are based on six earth systems, and they set boundaries within which each of these food systems can operate that will ensure the UN Sustainable Development Goals and the Paris Agreement are met (see Notes, page 57). Together they define sustainable food production, and it is the first time a globally agreed set of scientific targets has been devised – a major first, as to date the lack of this consensus has hampered progress in tackling climate change.

At a simplistic level, the targets aim to avoid the use of additional land for food production, to safeguard biodiversity, to reduce the consumption of water and manage it in an environmentally friendly way, to reduce nitrogen and phosphorus pollution, to produce zero carbon dioxide emissions and to avoid any increase in methane and nitrous oxide emissions (see page 238).

The Planetary Health Diet is the distillation of these, something like taking six loose strands of thread and bringing them together at one end. When these environmentally sustainable targets meet with a healthy way of eating, it creates the dynamic of a win-win diet. The idea is that this framework can be adapted to all food cultures, all production systems throughout the world, crucially with inbuilt flexibility to be adapted and scaled locally. The upshot? It will be possible to feed a healthy diet to the estimated global population of 10 billion people by 2050, within environmentally sustainable means.

WASTE NOT, WANT NOT

Whenever I read the dismaying figures about how much food households throw away every year, my immediate reaction is 'well, it's not me'; I cook everything from scratch and I work hard at recycling ingredients. But the 'not me' is an illusion, it is me, just as it is all of us, because in truth it is very difficult to avoid waste. And to whatever extent we may live by the old adage, 'waste not, want not', you have to really set your mind to it with a barrage of strategies, and even then, there are inevitably cracks between them. We all waste food for different reasons.

FIVE COMMON FOOD WASTE PITFALLS

Work-home balance

Even with a neat 9–5, many of us have an erratic work-home balance. This can result in thinking you will be eating at home when hunger descends, but ending up having something before you get there, because you're working late. Ditto the teenagers who have fuelled up at Subway on the way back from school. Uneaten suppers result.

Modern family life

The days of being expected to eat our greens, or whatever else fails to appeal, before being allowed to leave the table are by and large over. It is the new normal for everyone in a family to nurture different tastes. Many are the parents who find themselves cooking different meals at different times in the hope of getting something healthy down their offspring, rather than face a standoff at a family dinner. I know that I used to when my children were growing up.

The fridge

When I clear out the fridge, so often it is the half-jars of pesto and pasta sauce I chuck, the ravioli I bought in anticipation: convenience foods. And more half-jars of pickles and pastes, the tamarind, harissa and lemongrass paste, that pander to one particular culture without fitting in with others. All of these unhelpfully have different storage times, so their expiration date is easy to miss. The irony of the fridge is that at the same time as helping preserve foods, it also leads to waste. The trend for big fridges only exacerbates the problem.

Portion control

It's the leftover chocolate cake or cheesecake, which was enough to feed six, but we only had a sliver each and one was enough. And that extends to the packet of croissants. The habit, too, of cooking more than you need of food which cannot be reused.

Going on holiday

And then going on holiday, those final two days before we leave that cut a fine line between a fridge that looks like Mother Hubbard's cupboard and the depressing send-off of carrying out a sack of rubbish near full with food that will go off in the time we are away.

These are my personal pitfalls, and yours may be different. The point is, with a bit of effort I know I can do better. So this chapter is about creating awareness and looking for ways that we might be able to improve on the amount that we do throw out. This isn't about perfection; however hard we might try, there are times when it is unavoidable. Rather, by recognizing that waste is one of the greatest contributors by placing strain on global food security, and is one of the relatively few areas where we can make a real difference as consumers.

THE GLOBAL GOAL

The scientists behind the Planetary Health Diet have set the bar high, with the goal of at least halving food losses and waste globally. This would decrease the pressure on food demand, as well as reducing freshwater use and projected biodiversity loss. This waste runs from production through to consumption, and that is where we come in.

In highly developed countries, the public are responsible for a large proportion of food waste. And while it is not the easiest thing to quantify as a household, we should, through a mixture of behavioural changes and increased awareness, be able to help achieve that goal. So here are five ways in which we can potentially avoid waste. The goal is to make more of what we buy, and only buy what we need.

1. SHOPPING

Online or pop to the shops?

At any number of times of my life I have found online grocery shopping a complete lifesaver. The Covid-19 pandemic not least, but in advance of that, when my mother was elderly and unable to get out, a delivery service and the kindness of the driver in unpacking her shopping was as close as we had to community support. If you've just had a baby, or you are simply up against it, who would be without that buzz on the doorbell? But as a rule of thumb I do try to limit online grocery shopping to dried goods such as whole grains, pulses and nuts, and household goods like cleaning products, rather than fresh and perishable ingredients.

There is no substitute for actually choosing fresh ingredients ourselves. The loaf of bread that has a crust baked to your particular liking, fruit that is ripe in a way that fits with when you want to eat it, and crucially, fresh fish, poultry and meat: treats that deserve to be chosen with care. The Achilles heel of online services is under-ripe fruit, and perishable ingredients with a short shelf-life of 48 hours that allows little in the way of flexibility; you are much more likely to end up throwing them away than ingredients with a longer shelf-life you have selected yourself.

Little and often

Unless you are incredibly organized and do a weekly plan, over-shopping is much more likely to happen as a result of a massive once-weekly shop, than if you pop to the local store to buy supper for that day and the next. There is little to create symbiosis with your fridge like opening the door, realizing you have nothing for dinner and going out to buy it. Do this locally and on foot, and it is highly unlikely you will end up stocking up unnecessarily, not least because you have to carry it back home. With online shopping, I also quite often find myself buying a much bigger shop than I actually want, to meet the minimum basket total. Even worse, I tend to top it up with bottles of soft drinks or water that I don't even need, which are only adding to the overall recycling bin.

Make a list

I do love a list. My stack of lined A5 pads and royal blue Uni-balls might be a family joke, but I notice that everyone else in my family has also started using them, however much they ridicule such organization. A shopping list doesn't have to be too specific, but without one I either forget what I went for or come back with something I don't need. I always check the fridge before I shop, and at least then I can write '5 vegetables, 3 fruit', etc., to give some idea of quantity and planning.

Avoid ultra-processed foods

The hell of convenience comes in the form of a really long ingredient list, be it a pot noodle, a cereal, a sausage (including vegan), or a jar of pasta sauce. One where you have never heard of the majority of the ingredients listed, because most of them aren't food as such. For a nutritionist, ultra-processed foods are a horror story, where it is impossible to calculate what their nutritional value might be. Most such foods have very little by way of the nutrients that we need, consisting predominantly of the wrong kind of refined carbohydrates and fats, with too much salt, and chemicals masquerading as food. As well as being nutrient-poor, through usually being cheaper than

fresh ingredients, they contribute globally not only to obesity, but also to the anomaly of obesity and malnutrition existing side by side. But their other great sin is their contribution to waste.

Cook from scratch

One of the best ways of avoiding food waste is to cook from scratch. While nearly all primary ingredients can be recycled in some way, there is precious little that can be done with stale pizza, snacks or crisps, biscuits, iced buns or burgers. Careful planning and shopping for core ingredients, and keeping an eye on what you have in the fridge or cupboard, the veg basket and freezer, is the way to go in maximizing the food you buy. The fact that it is also central to good nutrition makes shopping and cooking from scratch a win-win scenario.

Redistribution

Consider downloading an app that covers your immediate area, for giving away any excess food you might have, especially following a party or over festive periods such as Christmas.

2. UNDERSTANDING USE BY AND BBE DATES

Use by = safety

'Use by' is the strict one, meaning the food is perishable. It normally refers to food that needs to be chilled at 5°C or lower, and needs to be eaten before this date to be safe. To this I would add trust your judgement. Poor transport conditions and storage can mean that a perishable foodstuff goes off before intended. If I am in any doubt, I don't eat it. And crucially, after this date, even if the food appears

to be OK, it should be discarded. The heartening news is that many perishable foods can be frozen. I aim to do this 48 hours in advance of their use by date to allow for defrosting (see Good freezer practice, page 30).

Best before (BBE – best before end of) date = quality

The 'Best before end of date' is the controversial one. It is intended as a guide to the quality of the food, and includes dried goods such as pasta and rice, spices, tinned foods, jams and condiments, and oils. But frequently, it results in a food getting chucked, when perhaps it needn't be. A food can deteriorate in flavour and texture, and some dried foods start to take longer to cook, but it doesn't suddenly go off in the month of January if that is what is specified, it could well be good for months beyond that. The exceptions I find are nuts and oils, which can go rancid, but you can taste for this without coming to harm.

BBE dates can be especially unhelpful in relation to fresh fruit and vegetables. All manner of fruit and veg can go on for weeks after the BBE date, such as apples, pears, lettuce, cabbages, butternut squash, celeriac and potatoes.

So the important thing is to exercise your judgement here. If you don't like the look or smell of a food, even if it is before its BBE date, bin it, and if it still seems good when the printed day of doom arrives, then there is no reason not to use it.

There are extremes, however. My mum was a part of the wartime generation of thrifty cooks, and never threw anything away. And when my brother and I were clearing out her kitchen after she died, many was the shriek of horror from behind a cupboard door as we unearthed some relish that should have been in a museum. And then there was our wedding cake. Traditionally, the idea was that you kept the second tier for the christening of your first child. Except that we kept ours for our second child, born eleven years after we married. Again, Miss Havisham springs to mind.

When I'm having a clear-out of dried goods or spices, I certainly wouldn't keep anything longer than a year, but months, yes. And even then, never say never, I have several spices that I know I cannot replace easily that have survived more than one cull.

Good fridge practice

I sometimes think my fridge rearranges itself. However hard I try to group ingredients by type, most mornings when I open the door it looks like it's had a rough night. Different fridges will have different temperature zones, the two constants are the bottom drawers which are warmer than the rest of the fridge and ideal for vegetables, salad and fruit, and boxes on the door are good for butter and Parmesan, and of course small jars. Try to position foods that need eating up at the front of the fridge, anything hidden at the back may well go off before you chance across it. And try to check everything every couple of days.

Good freezer practice

Any of these will be good popped into the freezer:

Milk
Butter
Yoghurt
Hard cheese
Meat
Poultry
Fish
Eggs – cracked and beaten
Bananas – peeled
Berries
Bread

Defrosting notes

Small cuts
Anything small, such as a fillet of fish, and bread will defrost within a couple of hours on the kitchen worktop.

Large cuts
My favourite way to defrost large items of food is to leave them inside a cast-iron casserole overnight, which not only protects the food from flies but also provides the perfect cool environment away from sunlight. Perfect for hot summer days too. Alternatively, start it off in the fridge overnight, and then remove it to the casserole or worktop the next day to finish defrosting. And obviously place it back in the fridge once it has.

Labelling
Label and date freezer foods, always. I've lost count of the times I've defrosted chicken stock thinking it was apple purée, and vice versa. Keeping a list on the freezer door with what you have is also a good way of making use of what you have and avoids white freezer fingers as you rummage through to the bottom of the drawers.

Eat it up
Try to eat the food within 24 hours of defrosting.

3. STORAGE TIPS

Storing bread

Unless I know that I have enough mouths to take care of a whole loaf, I always go for sliced bread (a good patisserie or bakery will do this to order) and keep it in the freezer. It toasts from frozen, with no loss of quality. Otherwise I cut big loaves in half or more, and freeze them, which only take an hour or two to defrost, but means you always have fresh bread at hand. Ditto baguettes, I keep out just enough for that day and freeze the remainder. Croissants and other breakfast breads that will be heated go straight into the freezer.

With this strategy there is no real need for endless ways of using up stale bread. But the tip for reviving a loaf nonetheless remains a favourite food hack (see Born-again bread, page 43).

Salad leaves and radishes

Always try to buy whole lettuces and prepare them just before you eat, any that's leftover can be stored in a lidded container in the bottom of the fridge and will be good the next day. There is much less waste this way than bags of salad leaves, especially if they are mixed, as they tend to deteriorate at different rates. The exception to a bagged salad is lamb's lettuce, rocket and baby spinach, which do keep well. Chicory and tight Little Gem hearts and Romaine lettuces are especially good keepers.

If, however, you do have salad leaves or radishes that are looking a little flaccid, they can be revived in a bowl or sink of cold water, with a few ice cubes, if you have some handy. Give them 20–30 minutes.

Stock

Stock is an ingredient that I religiously prepare following a roast, and religiously forget to use. It can of course be frozen, but in addition, at the five-day mark it can be brought to the boil, which will kill off any souring bacteria, and then kept for a further five days. In fact, you could do this ad infinitum, in the spirit of the eternal stews of old, that were kept simmering sometimes for years on end, and added to daily.

Storing fruit and veg

- All fruit and veg can be kept for longer in the fridge than out of it. Delicate fruits such as berries should be chilled regardless. Other fruits that have reached peak ripeness, and that you don't foresee eating straightaway, can be popped into the salad drawer.
- Separate out bananas from the rest of the fruit in a bowl, as gases given off will lead to the rapid ripening and spoilage of other fruits.
- Vegetables being stored in an airy basket at room temperature should have their plastic wrapping removed, which creates

a mini greenhouse and causes them to rot in no time. Ideally, try to buy them loose or bundled.

- Potatoes are supposed to be stored in a dark bag that can breathe to avoid their greening. However, at the risk of slightly sweetening if they are chilled when the starch turns to sugar, I do keep mine in the salad drawer in which case they will keep for an age. And given that they don't feature in a big way in this book (see Beyond potatoes, page 147), it is more than likely that you will need to keep them for a relatively long time.
- If you have excess herbs, try hanging them up in a small bunch in a dry area of the kitchen to dry. Mint is especially welcome as a tisane.

An excellent A–Z of how to store individual ingredients can be found at www.lovefoodhatewaste.com.

4. THE WHOLE FOOD

When you hear the phrase 'whole food' what does it conjure? I immediately think of brown rice, as opposed to white rice. As when the word first gained popularity, it was synonymous with refined versus unrefined grains, a byword for being rich in fibre, vitamins and minerals. But the true meaning of the word and its application to how we eat is very much broader and closely associated with food waste.

A key to eating in a planet-friendly fashion is to embrace the whole of the food. That starts when we are shopping, and continues in our preparation of ingredients, and eating them too.

Vegetables

The antithesis of whole vegetables is buying them trimmed and ready-prepared. The likelihood is that you will have to trim them all over again to remove browning sections, which is simply a waste of vegetable, and means they are nothing like as fresh as they would be if you prepared them yourself.

Instead seek them out in their whole state – carrots and beetroots with leaves and roots, Brussels sprouts on the stalk, tomatoes on the vine, mushrooms with soil clinging to their roots, the dirtier the potatoes the better, whole lettuces, lamb's lettuce with whiskery roots, radishes and watercress tied into a bunch, sweetcorn wrapped up in its husk and silk, whole cabbages. They will keep better, will likely be of a better quality, and it may be that some of the extras attached can also be eaten.

Another way of looking at it is that for the majority of vegetables, if there is no preparation involved then it isn't 'whole'. While trimming does involve some waste, a small compost bin is a great catch-all that can be used to recycle your ingredients.

Fruits

As with vegetables, avoid prepared fruits, which may have to be trimmed again, and deteriorate very much faster than the whole fruit. To get the full benefit, we want to eat as much of the fruit as possible, including apple and pear skins. Be aware of trends that sell themselves as convenience, such as tubs of pomegranate seeds that all too often are slightly fizzy by their use by date.

Meat, poultry and fish

There is certainly mileage in buying meat and poultry on the bone, if the bone goes on to provide the basis for a second meal, such as a stew or soup. But in relation to fish, buying the whole fish has more to do with an indication of its quality, than being greener per se. And if the idea of filleting and skinning fish is likely to make for eating it less, which is understandable, then it is much better to buy it ready-prepared.

Dried pulses, grains and nuts

Dried pulses are naturally whole, but the more popular grains will come in a range of finishes, from refined to polished and whole. Try to choose polished or whole over refined. But again, if you have children, for instance, who might settle for half refined and half whole grain, at least that is progress if the alternative is simply the refined ingredient.

On a personal note, I wish I had started my children on whole grains younger. As it is, bringing them up before good nutrition was at the fore, I indulged them in refined pasta, bread and rice and it is an ongoing battle today to get everyone in my family on the same page. The majority of fast foods, such as burgers and pizzas, also tend to be served up as refined products, which does unfortunately give such foods a glamorous edge in children's eyes. It may be worth countering this by making these foods at home using wholegrain products.

5. PREPPING

Going back to my very earliest days of cooking, the lot of a commis chef was to prepare the vegetables all day in a restaurant kitchen. Perhaps the fiddliest task of all was the tomatoes. First a small cone was nicked from the top to remove the stalk, next they were lowered into a pan of boiling water for about 20 seconds and then into a pan of cold water so that the skins could be cut off. They were then deseeded before being finely diced. And without knowing better, nearly all my early recipes recommend doing just this. I blush with shame.

The sheer waste of all those antioxidants and bioactive compounds and fibre. These days I treasure tomatoes for their skin, their seeds and their flesh, so that's one less fiddly task to grapple with.

Skins

- The skins of potatoes, carrots and beetroot are flavourful and nutritious, especially when roasted or baked, and contribute both fibre and micronutrients.
- Onion skins can add flavour to stock, and likewise garlic cloves can be roasted or simmered skin-on.

- Be sure to eat the skins of apples, pears, plums, peaches and nectarines.

Leaves

- Outer lettuce leaves may be too tough for the salad bowl, but rid them of browning bits and they can be wilted in a pan with a little oil, garlic, ginger and chilli, like a Chinese cabbage.
- Carrot tops and beetroot tops can be added to soups and stews.
- Broad bean tops and pea tops, if you chance across them, are deliciously light salad material.

Outer layers and pips

- The outer sticks of celery and sheathes of fennel may be too stringy to eat as they are, but they can still be cooked and pressed through a sieve for a soup or purée. Or save them for the stock pot.
- When I am making a fruit purée, such as apple or pear, I cook the whole of the fruit and then press it through a sieve, which is less wasteful (and saves time) than trimming before cooking.

Stalks

- Fine soft-herb stalks such as parsley and coriander can be chopped or puréed and have just as much flavour as the leaves, with less fiddly picking over too.
- The toughened stalks of broccoli, cauliflower and asparagus are great for smooth soups that are sieved.

MY TOP TEN STORAGE TIPS

1. Narrow your flavour palate

The modern approach to cooking at home is to skip around the world, Indian one night, Mexican another, Thai the next. But this is a sure-fire route to waste. Think twice before buying multiple spices, condiments and pastes that will only get an occasional outing, as they are almost bound to end up as landfill. Instead, I prefer to cook good simple food and let the ingredients themselves star.

2. Cut down on oils

Try not to have five on the go at once. Extra virgin olive oil is essential, I keep a basic for cooking and another slightly more special one for dressings. Rapeseed is also an excellent all-rounder and groundnut too. But the avocado, walnut and hazelnut, and anything flavoured, often goes to waste in my kitchen, so now I avoid buying them.

Store oils in a dark cupboard to extend their shelf-life and try to buy them in dark glass bottles. As outlined on page 29, use the Best before end (BBE) date as a guide to quality, there is no issue if they have lost a little of their flavour, and it is easy enough to tell if they have started to turn rancid just by smelling.

3. Cut down on condiments

Store these in the fridge, and as above, try to restrict yourself to just one or two flavour palates. In the case of chutneys and pickles, open a jar at a time, and try to finish it.

4. Freeze fresh coffee and spices

Coffee

I keep my ground coffee in the freezer to keep it fresh. You can also freeze coffee beans.

Spices

For those spices that oxidize quickly, such as paprika and cayenne, the freezer is the best place to store them. Or, if you see that a spice is approaching its BBE date, then you can pop it into the freezer. Very few spices go off as such, but they do lose and change flavour.

5. Keep an eye on the nuts in your cupboard

I confess to throwing away a lot of nuts, it is one ingredient where I span the range. My solution is the recipe on page 45, which will also do for any mixture of nuts. As well as providing a snack they can be sprinkled over salads and soups, which helps in reducing our intake of animal protein, increasing our plant protein.

6. Good dairy practice

Milk

While the dietary allowance for milk (see page 16) is for whole milk, it is worth noting that skimmed milk keeps better than full-fat, as well as being the recommendation for this diet. Filtered milk also contains less of the souring bacteria that can spoil milk. Otherwise, little and often, I generally buy milk by the pint rather than the huge 4-pint cartons, unless I am sure that I will be using it. And, of course, it freezes.

Cheese

The best route to avoiding waste here is to have only one or two on the go at once. Make sure they are protected so as to avoid drying out; waxed food wraps are ideal. If a cheese like Cheddar develops mould, simply slice this off. And be mindful of fresh curd and cream cheeses, which tend to spoil more quickly. Parmesan will keep almost indefinitely.

7. Cherish those half dozen eggs

While eggs are a commonly wasted food, within the recommendations they are a special treat, and as such less likely to go to waste. Buy them half a dozen at a time, and if they do go beyond their BBE date, it isn't the end of the world, treat yourself to a small omelette, or whisk and freeze them.

8. The fruit bowl

I only keep as much fruit as I know can be eaten within a few days in the fruit bowl. The rest I store in the fridge. Also, if something is starting to ripen, such as a banana or avocado, but I can't foresee

using them within 24 hours, then again, I pop them into the fridge. And if I do suddenly have an excess, then I make a fruit purée and freeze it in batches.

9. Freeze fresh meat

Only keep out as much meat as you are likely to eat within about 48 hours, and freeze any more than this. And try to freeze meat at least 48 hours before its use by date, given the time that will be required to defrost it (see Good freezer practice, page 30).

10. Buy frozen fish

I buy a lot of my fish frozen, with the exception of salmon, mackerel and shellfish. I also often take advantage of salmon when it is plentiful, and buy a whole side and portion and freeze it. Frozen fish is frequently fresher than what is on the fishmonger's slab, and it then serves as a convenience, taking no more than a couple of hours to defrost.

RICHES FROM THE SCRAPS

The trick to being resourceful with ingredients that might get thrown away is to use them in dishes you are sure will get eaten. This may sound obvious, but the danger of a bread and butter pudding, quiche or banana loaf is the possibility of creating more waste if there are not enough people to eat them.

So I wanted to give you a handful of recipes that I find really useful, that I have turned to again and again over the years as my favourite ways of using up common ingredients.

I find potential waste tends to collect around hotspots in my kitchen: the vegetable basket, the fruit bowl, the fridge and salad drawers, and the bread bin. Here are my key recipes for each of them.

SERVES 4

READY IN 30–40 MINUTES

VEGETARIAN

GOOD FOR

THE VEG BASKET

FRIDGE ODDS AND ENDS

STOCK

TOUGH VEGETABLE TRIMMINGS

RICHES FROM THE RUBBLE SOUP

This one soup recipe will take care of pretty much any odd veg you have going and need to use up, be it raw or cooked, as well as stock, and any snippets of leftover chicken or meat, lentils, grains, pasta and the like. And every time you make it, the soup will be completely different, which is one of its charms.

2 tbsp extra virgin olive oil
1 medium white or yellow onion, chopped, or 2 banana shallots, chopped
2 garlic cloves, peeled and finely chopped (optional)
500g raw veggies (600–700g untrimmed), chopped, such as carrots, parsnips, celeriac, pumpkin, butternut squash, peas, broccoli, leeks, cauliflower, asparagus, mushrooms, red peppers, celery, potatoes
150ml vegetarian white wine
approximately 750ml vegetable stock (see opposite)
sea salt and freshly ground black pepper

SERVING IDEAS

chopped flat-leaf parsley or coriander
snipped chives
soured cream
drizzle of extra virgin olive oil
freshly grated vegetarian Parmesan-style cheese
crispy wholemeal croutons

1. Heat the oil in a medium or large saucepan and fry the onion or shallots for about 5 minutes until softened, stirring frequently. Add the garlic just before the end if wished.

2. Add the chopped vegetables and fry these for a couple of minutes.

3. Add the white wine and simmer until reduced by half.

4. Add the stock to cover the vegetables by a couple of centimetres. Bring this to the boil, add plenty of sea salt and black pepper, and simmer for 10–20 minutes until the veggies are soft.

VARIATIONS

Creamed Purée the soup in batches in a blender, and if necessary, press through a sieve.

Textured Purée the soup in batches in a food processor.

Hearty rustic Make sure your vegetables are cut quite small in the first place. Purée half the soup in a food processor, then add back to the rest.

Stew-like Leave the veggies whole. Great for adding leftover snippets – chicken, meat, cooked lentils, grains or pasta, and other cooked veggies.

READY IN 25–30 MINUTES

VEGETARIAN

GOOD FOR

THE VEG BASKET

TOUGH VEGETABLE TRIMMINGS

VEGETABLE STOCK

Any mix of veggies is good here, but if you want to proceed to make a mash (see page 42), then they will need to be trimmed and prepped. Allowing for evaporation, you should end up with about ¾ of the amount of water that you add.

- approximately 1kg raw veggies, diced (prepared weight), such as carrot, leek, celery, onion, fennel, swede, celeriac, tomato
- 2 garlic cloves, peeled and finely chopped
- 150ml vegetarian white wine

continued overleaf ▶

a few sprigs of fresh thyme
sea salt and freshly ground black pepper

1. Place all the ingredients in a large saucepan, and cover with water by about 3cm (1¼in). Bring to the boil, and simmer over a low heat for 15 minutes.

2. Strain, reserving the stock, leave this to cool, then cover and chill until required.

VEGGIE MASH

You can make even more of the above recipe by turning the veg into a mash after straining the stock – purée them with butter or olive oil and soft green herbs such as parsley or chives and season.

TOMATO AND BREAD SALAD

SERVES 4

READY IN 1 HOUR 15 MINUTES–1 HOUR 45 MINUTES

VEGETARIAN

GOOD FOR

THE BREAD BIN

OVER-RIPE TOMATOES

Of all the ways of using up slightly stale bread, this has to be my favourite, ushering us to a shaded table in Tuscany or Umbria.

700g flavourful ripe tomatoes, cored and cut into 2–3cm (¾–1¼in) dice
flaky sea salt
1 tsp caster sugar
6 tbsp extra virgin olive oil, plus extra for drizzling
1 tbsp red wine vinegar
approximately 270g slightly stale bread (e.g. ciabatta or sourdough), crusts removed and torn into 2–3cm (¾–1¼in) chunks
100g pitted green or black olives
6 tbsp coarsely chopped flat-leaf parsley

1. Place the tomatoes in a bowl, toss with 1 level teaspoon of salt and the sugar and set aside for 30 minutes.

2. Drain the tomatoes into a sieve, collecting the juice in a bowl below. Add the oil and vinegar to the bowl and stir to make a dressing.

3. Place the bread in a large serving bowl, sprinkle over the dressing, half at a time, to soak it evenly, and set aside until it has been absorbed.

4. Toss the tomatoes and olives into the bread. Cover and set aside for 30–60 minutes for the bread to soften further, then gently mix in the parsley, and check for seasoning. Splash over some more oil before serving.

BORN-AGAIN BREAD

One of my favourite hacks is for slightly stale baguettes and bread loaves: they can be brought back to life by briefly passing them under the cold tap and then heating them in a medium oven until the crust has crisped, while the inside returns to being soft and fluffy. A baguette takes 10 minutes at 190°C (fan 170°C/gas mark 5). Rolls and half-loaves can also be revived (warming time may vary).

HERB PURÉE

MAKES 200G
READY IN 5 MINUTES
VEGAN

GOOD FOR
BUNCHES OF SOFT HERBS

This purée is lovely in any number of scenarios, with curries and stews, stirred through vegetable purée or soup. You can vary the quantity of the individual herbs. Flat-leaf parsley works well too.

20g coriander leaves
20g mint leaves

continued overleaf ▶

20g basil leaves
8 tbsp extra virgin olive oil
2–3 tsp lemon or lime juice
1 tsp chopped medium-hot green chilli
1 tsp chopped shallot
sea salt, to taste

1. Place all the ingredients in a food processor and whizz to a thick green sauce.

GOOD FOR
THE FRUIT BOWL
LEFTOVER YOGHURT
LEFTOVER FRUIT JUICE

BREAKFAST SMOOTHIES

Smoothies are a great way to use any fruit that needs eating up, or that might have started to turn, when you can cut out the bad bits and whizz up the good bits. Use these as a blueprint.

SERVES 2
READY IN 5 MINUTES
VEGETARIAN

BERRY BANANA SMOOTHIE

2 tbsp Greek yoghurt
200ml smooth fruit juice, e.g. orange, apple, grapefruit or pomegranate
150g berries, e.g. blueberries, raspberries, strawberries or blackberries
2 small bananas, peeled and cut into chunks

1. Place all the ingredients in a blender and whizz until smooth, then divide between two highball glasses.

SERVES 2
READY IN 5 MINUTES
VEGETARIAN

EXOTIC SMOOTHIE

1 banana, peeled and cut into chunks
½ papaya or mango, peeled, stoned and roughly chopped
300ml smooth fruit juice, e.g. orange, apple, grapefruit or pomegranate
a couple of dollops of Greek yoghurt and seeds of 1 passionfruit, to serve (optional)

1. Whizz the first three ingredients in a blender until smooth. Divide between 2 glasses. Serve with a dollop of yoghurt and topped with passionfruit seeds, if wished.

ROASTED SEEDS

MAKES 200G
READY IN 1 HOUR
VEGAN

GOOD FOR
THE STORE CUPBOARD

This is my go-to for the all the odds and ends of packets of leftover seeds. This is the seed version, but nuts (using the same method) are just as good, as is a mixture.

1 tsp vegetable oil
100g pumpkin seeds
60g sunflower seeds
40g sesame seeds
2 tsp tamari sauce
2 tsp maple syrup
2 tsp lemon juice
pinch of cayenne pepper

1. Preheat the oven to 150°C (fan 130°C/gas mark 2). Brush the base of a large roasting tin with the oil. Combine all the seeds in a medium bowl and spread in a thin layer over the base. Roast for 20 minutes.

2. Blend the remaining ingredients in a small bowl. Drizzle over the seeds, stir to coat and then roast for another 30 minutes, stirring halfway through. Loosen with a spatula and leave to cool. Transfer to an airtight container. They will keep well for several weeks.

SERVES 4

READY IN 20–30 MINUTES

VEGETARIAN

GOOD FOR

OVER-RIPE BANANAS

USING UP MILK

LEFTOVER YOGHURT

THE ODD EGG

BANANA PANCAKES WITH MAPLE SYRUP

Speedier than banana bread, these pancakes rely on the same slightly blackened and heady fruits as the cake. They are also a good way of spreading the egg allowance. Of the many syrups out there, maple and date are personal favourites, or a resinous honey.

2 very ripe small bananas
1 quantity of batter recipe (see Simply pancakes, page 75)
5g unsalted butter

TO SERVE

Greek yoghurt or soured cream
maple or date syrup
finely chopped walnuts

1. Mash the bananas in a medium bowl, then gradually pour in the batter and blend.

2. Heat a 24cm (9½in) non-stick frying pan over a medium heat, add the butter for the first pancake and swirl to melt, then add a quarter of the pancake mixture and tip the pan to spread it over the base. Fry for about 1 minute until the underside is golden, then turn and fry the topside for another 30–60 seconds. Slip onto a plate and cook 3 more pancakes in the same fashion.

3. Serve with a dollop of yoghurt or soured cream spread in the middle, drizzle with plenty of syrup, and scatter with nuts.

GRAINOLOGY

60% WHOLE GRAINS

Transforming our carb intake will, for many of us, be one of the biggest challenges of eating to support the planet. Complex carbohydrates, that consist of many sugar molecules joined together, are our primary source of energy. But while a Westernized diet has traditionally looked to potatoes as a staple, these are now rationed at 50g a day on the Planetary Health Diet, and instead we need to aim to consume some 60 per cent of our energy in the form of whole grains. This inevitably means cutting right back on refined grains and related products – white rice, pasta, couscous and bread to boot – and choosing instead their unrefined equivalents.

So whole grains, in all their variety, are very much in the spotlight. Most of us will have one or two favourites that we turn to on a regular basis, but beyond that, I know that I personally am inclined to get stuck in a rut, instead of taking advantage of the wide

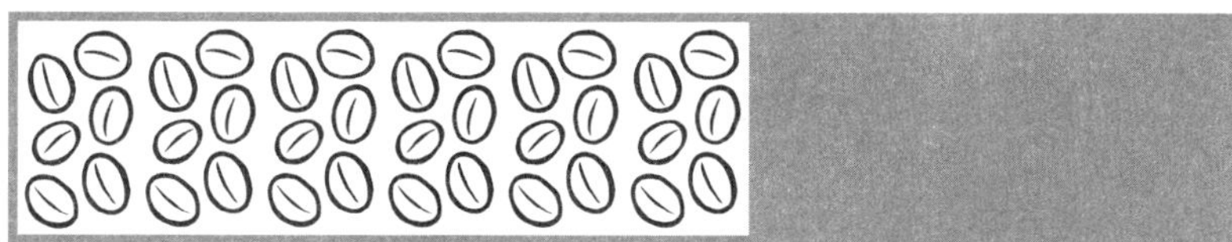

60% OF OUR ENERGY SHOULD COME FROM WHOLE GRAINS

spectrum on offer. But eating for sustainability means broadening out the range of grains we eat. Some of the lesser-known varieties can be cultivated with fewer fertilizers and pesticides than modern breeds, given that they haven't been bred with specific traits in mind. At a nutritional level, the best way to treat grains is as you might vegetables; each one will have a slightly different profile, so eating across the board affords the best possible scope of nutrients.

REFINED V. WHOLE?

Why would you eat a food that has all the natural goodness stripped out of it? Why would you remove the fibre, the micronutrients, or vitamins and minerals? This question haunts nutritionists, given how illogical it is. We consume piles of white rice and then take vitamin pills to make up for the lack of nutrition, or even more ironic, enrich refined grains by adding vitamins back in, but in a different proportion – just think of all those breakfast cereals boasting the addition of vitamins. It just doesn't make sense. It's not as though one is more expensive than the other. Whole grains may take longer to cook, but even that's not an argument when increasingly we can buy them ready-cooked or quick cook.

Familiarity will account for a large part of any preference for refined grains, if you have grown up eating white rice, white pasta and white bread; old habits die hard. In practice whole grains have much more character, taste and a better texture than their bland refined counterparts. So a lot of this will have to do with reconditioning or changing our expectations. But as anyone who has tried to cut down on sugar will know, it is no time before the sweet treats you previously enjoyed seem unpalatable, so with a little time and patience, it is a switch that will be well-rewarded.

WHAT IS A REFINED GRAIN?

Refined grains are little more than sugar, stripped of their fibre and micronutrients. Instead of slowly releasing sugar into the bloodstream along with vitamins and minerals, they cause sugar spikes, which in turn can lead us to rapidly feel hungry again and craving the wrong sorts of foods.

WHAT IS A WHOLE GRAIN?

Whole grain means just that, the entire grain seed: the bran, the germ and the endosperm, which between them contain all the naturally occurring nutrients the grain has to offer, in the original proportions. They can still be cracked, crushed or rolled, providing they retain the original balance of nutrients. But, if such a process resulted in a change in proportion, more endosperm or bran for instance, then it would have to forego its coveted status. And unlike refined grains, the sugar is very gradually released into the blood making for a sustained release of energy.

Bran

The bran is best known for containing fibre, but also contains antioxidants and B vitamins, and provides a protective coating for the germ and endosperm.

Germ

The germ is the seed within the grain, from which it sprouts, and contains some protein and healthy fats in addition to B vitamins and minerals.

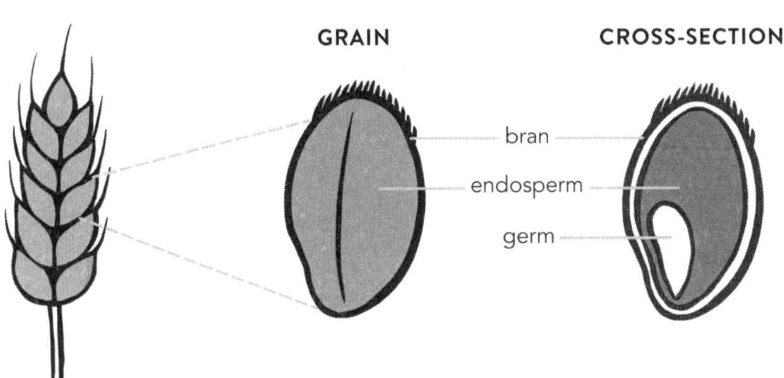

Endosperm

The endosperm is what we know, for instance, as white rice or flour. Within nature, it nurtures the germ as a food supply. It is best known for its starchy carbohydrates and contains some protein and a modest number of vitamins and minerals. By removing the bran and germ when a grain is refined, you strip away anything up to two thirds of some nutrients, as well as the fibre and some protein.

WHAT IS A POLISHED GRAIN?

Certain grains, in particular spelt and barley, are 'polished' or pearled. Although technically this involves some refining by removing the bran, their fibre is distributed throughout the grain, so the polished or pearled varieties still have significantly more fibre than say, white rice. Pearled spelt, for instance, has about four times the amount of fibre than white rice.

It is unusual to find spelt and barley in their 'whole' form, as they tend to take longer to cook and be tougher to eat. So in the recipes that follow, it is the polished or pearled varieties that are suggested.

A HANDY SUPPLY

Because whole grains are so central to this way of eating, I like to pre-cook a batch to have on hand in the fridge – easily turning this nutritious powerhouse into a convenience food. If they are there at the ready, I find I am much more likely to throw a handful into whatever I am cooking or preparing.

And they are surprisingly adaptable. I know that we tend to think of them as the healthy equivalent of eating white rice, and I do wonder if that is to their disadvantage, as given their robust character they are not always suited to being served as a side. I prefer to use them little and often, which lightens their presence. You will find throughout the book that any number of dishes, such as salads, omelettes, soups and stews, have been bolstered with a smattering here and there.

COOKING WHOLE GRAINS

There is no need to soak whole grains. Instead rinse them under the cold tap in a sieve before boiling in a plentiful amount of unsalted water. Start testing them a few minutes before the suggested cooking time, and once they are just tender, drain them into a sieve.

Hot

Set the sieve over the saucepan and leave for a few minutes to steam-dry before serving.

Cold

Run the sieve under the cold tap to stop the cooking process, then transfer to a bowl, cover, leave to cool and then chill straightaway. They will keep for a couple of days. Either use cold in dishes, stir-fry or stir into soups or stews.

WHOLE GRAIN ROUNDUP

Barley

Barley is one of the oldest cultivated grains. Many of us have grown up with it as the comforting carb in an Irish stew, but its talents extend well beyond this. It makes for a delicious risotto and is a great way of padding out a salad. It is usually sold 'pearled'.

Einkorn

This niche strain of wheat is considered to be the most ancient of all. Use it as you would spelt or farro (in France it is *petit épeautre*, little spelt, and in Italy *farro piccolo*, little farro), although cooking times may differ. As a wheat that is hard to hull, it is more likely to be found whole than spelt and farro, which are usually pearled. It also thrives in areas of low fertility, so potentially has value in drought-prone regions.

Farro/Emmer (*Triticum turgidum dicoccum*)

Italy leads the charge here, where emmer is known as *grano farro* or *farro medio*. An ancient strain of wheat, it has avoided the

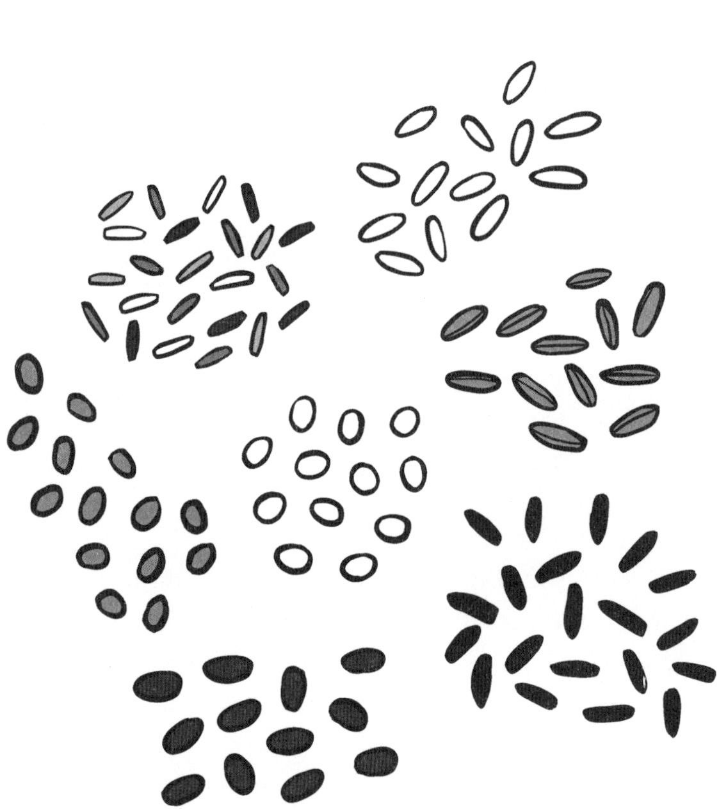

hybridization of modern wheats, and preceded the popularity of durum wheat, which is more easily hulled, and has a gluten content that provides the structure for bread. Like einkorn and spelt, it has a deliciously nutty savour and toothsome texture.

Millet

Millet is a common name for several related grains that all perform in the same way. This tiny mustard-coloured grain cooks up like a porridge with an appealing bitterness. If you are unfamiliar with it, then the Spinach and millet porridge with cashews (page 200) is a good place to start. Like other ancient grains, these have been consumed for thousands of years in many regions of the world. They form the principal staple grain in India, eaten in many different forms.

Rice

One of the three global grain staples, alongside corn and wheat. Brown rice is the wholegrain version of what we eat as white rice. Red and black rice are two personal favourites, niche wholegrain rices that can be used interchangeably. However, in relation to sustainability, rice paddies are also associated with methane gas emissions, which impact on climate change, so it is a grain to eat occasionally.

Rye

Because of its ability to thrive in cold and wet areas, rye has a considerable presence in Northern Europe and Russia – think of all the beautiful dark rye breads. Unusually its endosperm has an especially high level of fibre, in addition to that in the bran, which gives rye a lower glycaemic index than many other grains and makes it a good choice for diabetics. Most of the rye we see for sale comes in the form of flakes, which are best suited to breakfast cereal dishes. Look out for the whole grain sold as 'berries'; delectably nutty, I treat them almost as I would chopped nuts.

Spelt (*Triticum aestivum spelta*)

Considered a closely related subspecies of common wheat, spelt is one of three ancient wheats that come under the 'farro' banner. In Italy it is grown as *farro grande* or big farro. Unlike modern wheat varieties, it hasn't been bred and hybridized in the same way as newer varieties and is regarded as a purer ingredient. Most of what we can buy is 'pearled' spelt.

Teff

This African staple, a type of millet, is the main source of nutrition for over two-thirds of Ethiopians, and is commonly eaten in Eritrea and the Horn of Africa. It has tiny, tiny grains, usually grey in colour, although it does come in several hues, and it cooks to a porridge-like consistency, and is also used for flatbreads and in other baking.

Wheat

Wheat takes pride of place within the grain family as our staple. Its gluten content provides the structure for loaves, without which it is difficult to achieve a good rise. While pasta relies on durum wheat, bread wheat forms the basis of most other baked products. It is divided into hard wheat, that has a higher protein content than soft wheat and more gluten, making it ideal for bread, and soft wheat, with its lower protein content, making it better suited to cakes and biscuits. There are further divisions of spring and winter varieties, depending on when they are sown, and also the colour of the kernels can differ in being red or white.

For the purposes of this book, our interest lies with wholewheat pasta and bread, bulgur wheat, and also wheat berries, which can sometimes be cracked to speed the cooking time.

Wild rice

This aquatic grass was traditionally grown by the tribes around the Great Lakes of North America. It has long, thin black grains that when cooked retain a firm chewy bite, and are often mixed with other grains to mitigate this. Treat them as you might nuts, just a handful of grains added in with softer ingredients is the way to go, which is why it is quite often mixed into white or brown basmati rice.

FAVOURITE GRAIN PRODUCTS

Bulgur

Bulgur wheat is a processed product, boiled, dried and ground, but still counts as a whole grain. The advantage lies with its speed of preparation: many recipes call merely for it to be soaked rather than cooked. It is the bedrock of tabbouleh and makes great pilafs.

Corn

Consumed globally as tortillas, polenta and popcorn. Be sure that the packaging for cornmeal and polenta advertises that the whole grain has been used.

Freekeh

A personal favourite, the wheat is harvested green before being roasted; it has a gorgeously deep, savoury, smoky scent.

Oats

Stone-ground oatmeal goes well beyond porridge, for fillings and coating foods for frying. The nutritional USP lies with beta-glucan fibre that is known to help lower cholesterol.

FAUX GRAINS

There are a handful of grains that we treat as honorary members of the club. Amaranth, buckwheat and quinoa are all pseudo-grains: they are grasses and not truly part of the *Poaceae* botanical family. But, because they have similar nutritional profiles and we cook and eat them in the same way, they are generally classified as whole grains. All three of these pseudo-grains can boast higher levels of protein than other grains, and are complete proteins, containing all nine essential amino acids.

Amaranth

We don't hear a great deal about this diminutive little grain. About the size of quinoa, it has a more pronounced flavour, quite peppery. But try it for size where you might usually eat quinoa. It has a higher level of protein than most other grains, at 13–14 per cent. Its cultivation goes back some 6,000–8,000 years and it was a staple crop for the Aztecs. Most importantly, it is a highly adaptive crop that grows in almost any elevation and any temperate climate, thriving in low-water conditions, which makes it especially valuable for drought-prone regions.

Buckwheat

One of my favourite grains, this is related to sorrel, knotweed and rhubarb. It is a real nutritional powerhouse, with a biological value above 90 per cent (the proportion that can be actively used by the body), courtesy of the high concentration of all the essential amino acids. Blinis, Breton crêpes and Japanese soba noodles all owe their charm to buckwheat. The pretty triangular groats have a mild mushroom flavour and are great in all manner of salads in place of rice or pasta. Environmentally, it has the advantage of growing in poor soil and thriving without chemical pesticides.

Quinoa

The best known of the pseudo-grains, quinoa is the edible seeds of a species of goosefoot, a flowering plant in the amaranth family. The fine C-shaped tail or germ that separates out from the seed when it cooks gives it a uniquely delicate texture, and despite its small size, it always retains a slight bite. These days it can be found in different colours: red, purple and black, often sold as a mix. It is one of the grains you are most likely to encounter in pre-cooked form.

NOTES

1. Walter Willett, Johan Rockström, Brent Loken, et al., 'Food in the Anthropocene: The EAT-*Lancet* Commission on healthy diets from sustainable food systems', *Lancet* vol. 393 (2 February 2019), pp. 447–92. The Anthropocene is the current geological age: it is defined as the period during which human activity has had an environmental impact on the earth.
2. *Ibid.*, p. 447.
3. <https://www.bhf.org.uk/informationsupport/heart-matters-magazine/news/coronavirus-and-your-health/what-makes-you-at-risk-from-coronavirus> accessed 23 July 2020.
4. The UN Sustainable Development Goals (SDGs) seek to end poverty, protect the planet, ensure prosperity for all, and eradicate hunger and malnourishment.
5. The Paris Agreement focuses on climate change and its effects on human health. Limiting global warming to well below 2°C, aiming for 1.5°C, is not possible by only decarbonizing the global energy system. To reach this goal, what is required is both transitioning to food systems that can provide negative emissions (i.e. function as a major carbon sink instead of a major carbon source) and protecting carbon sinks in natural ecosystems.
6. EAT, *Healthy Diets From Sustainable Food Systems: Food, Planet, Health* (Summary Report of the EAT-*Lancet* Commission, 2019), p. 10 <eatforum.org/content/uploads/2019/07/EAT-Lancet_Commission_Summary_Report.pdf> accessed 4 November 2020.
7. Professor Walter Willett, interview with the author (23 March 2020).

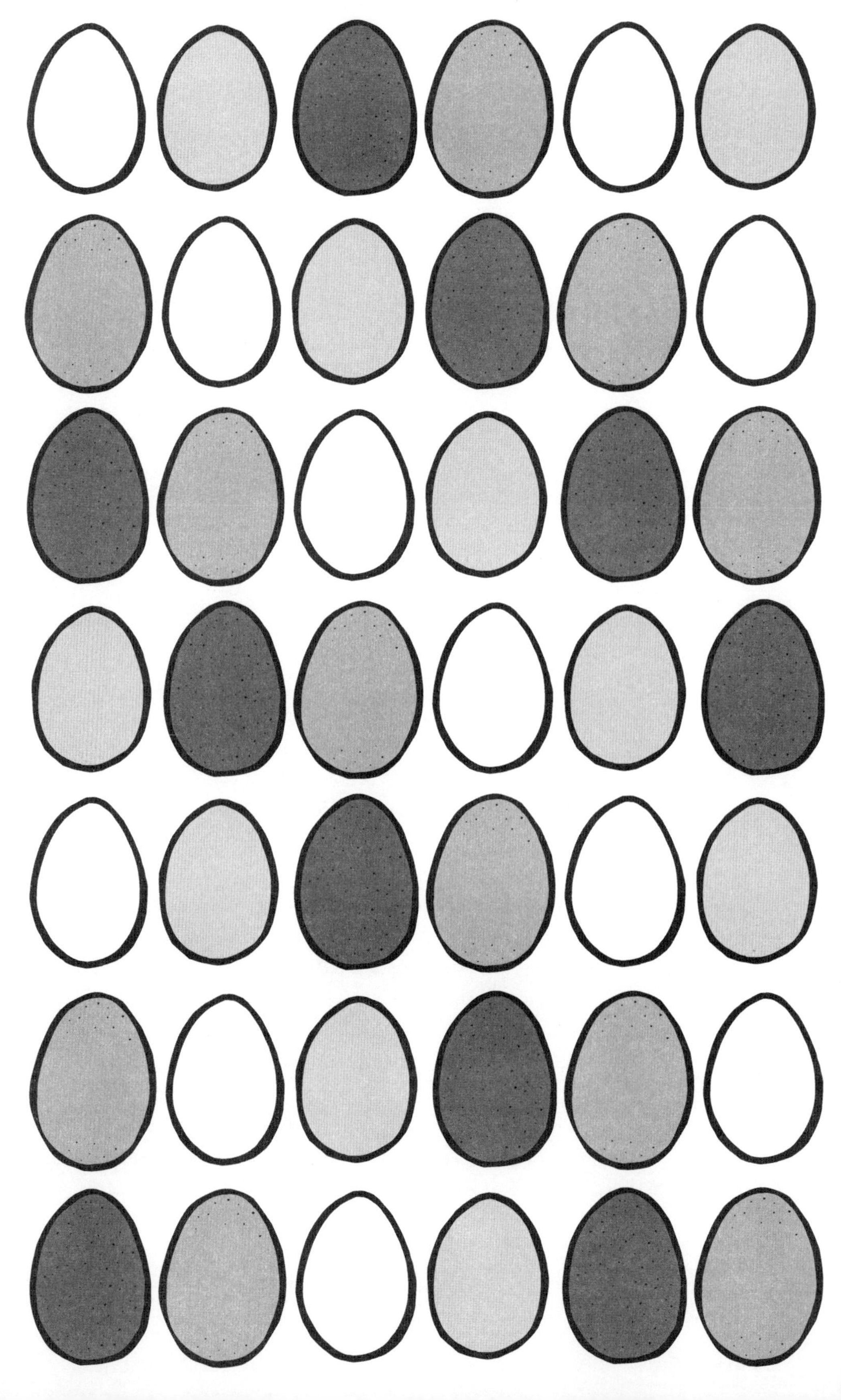

ONE EGG DISHES

THE PORCELAIN SHEEN OF A FEW EGGS IN A WIRE RACK ON MY kitchen worktop is as essential to my sense of well-being as knowing there is enough bread to go with the eggs. I don't buy them with any particular game plan in mind, it is not a case of 'if', but when. Guaranteed, at least twice a week, when I can't quite muster the energy to cook a proper supper, or when someone in the household needs a speedy resolution to gnawing hunger on their way out of the door, or back in again, and it's just the one person, they amount to frying pan gold. Free-range eggs are a comfort blanket, and as convenient as high-quality animal protein gets.

The Planetary Health Diet recommends an optional 13g of egg per day, which sizes up to 1½ a week (something only a computer could come up with!). So let us round that figure to just the one large free-range egg a week. Not much I know, the equivalent of wartime rations of one tin of dried egg every two months. But, at least we get to enjoy them fresh. And it is only when pushed that you realise just how many great dishes you can create with so little. Having less isn't in itself a bad thing here, as it means that what is lacking in quantity opens the door to other plant-based ingredients, be that grains, legumes or fresh vegetables, to fill the gap.

Eggs have, as might be expected, the same environmental footprint as chicken. The projected recommended output by 2050 doesn't actually differ hugely from today; what is needed, however, is a global reallocation in consumption. In North America and Europe we consume roughly double the amount recommended, while in South Asia and Sub-Saharan Africa, an egg could significantly improve the nutritional quality of a child's diet, and therefore the stunting of growth, by replacing calories from a refined starchy food with the equivalent of a high-quality protein.

The advice on how many eggs we should be eating from a nutritional perspective fluctuates with the science, but one positive about only eating one egg a week is that we are highly unlikely to run into health issues. So let us cherish this one egg by making it the centre of attention in the dishes that follow. Two eggs sunny-side up may be off the menu as a daily breakfast, but their sheer versatility means we can continue to welcome them into our week as an occasional treat.

SERVES 2

READY IN 35–45 MINUTES

VEGETARIAN

PISSALADIÈRE OMELETTE

approximately 2 tbsp extra virgin olive oil
2 medium white or yellow onions, peeled, halved and thinly sliced
sea salt and freshly ground black pepper
2 tbsp tomato passata rustica
2 large free-range eggs
50g cooked freekeh, spelt or brown rice
30g pitted dried black olives, halved

Pizza omelettes are a great way of enjoying our one egg a week (see page 17), where a wafer-thin omelette replaces the usual refined bread base. So let your mind wander to all your preferred pizza toppings – and a Pissaladière, one of my personal favourites among this genre, is a variation on the theme. There's no missing the anchovies in this plant-powered version, which is boosted with whole grains in the omelette base. Try to use dried black olives, spliced with herbs, otherwise you could add a teaspoon of fresh thyme or marjoram leaves to the onions as they stew.

1. Add 1 tablespoon of oil and 2 tablespoons of water to a small non-stick saucepan, add the onions, scatter over ½ teaspoon of sea salt and stir. Cover with a lid and cook over a low heat for 25–35 minutes, stirring occasionally until the onions are syrupy and almost jam-like.

2. Meanwhile, stir 1 teaspoon of oil into the tomato rustica in a small bowl and season it. In another small bowl, whisk the eggs with a little seasoning, then stir in the grains.

3. Preheat the grill to high. Preheat a 24cm (9½in) non-stick frying pan, with a heatproof handle, over a medium heat. Add 1 teaspoon of oil to the frying pan, then tip in the eggs and grains and evenly spread over the base of the pan. Cook for 1–2 minutes until sizzling around the edges and golden underneath. At the same time, drizzle over the tomato rustica, spread with the onions and scatter over the olives.

4. Pop under the grill for 2–3 minutes or until golden, sizzling and puffy around the outside.

SERVES 2

READY IN 15–20 MINUTES

VEGETARIAN

SPINACH AND SCAMORZA PIZZA OMELETTE

120g cherry tomatoes, halved or quartered
sea salt and freshly ground black pepper
2 large free-range eggs
50g cooked spelt or freekeh
2 tsp extra virgin olive oil
1 garlic clove, peeled and crushed to a paste
200g baby spinach leaves
50g scamorza or drained cow's milk mozzarella, thinly sliced
15g pine nuts

This is another pizza-style omelette (see page 62), that marries cheese and spinach. Scamorza, which makes for a particular treat, brings back memories of a small trattoria clinging to a mountain hillside in Italy while sipping on a Campari and soda, which is how I met and fell in love with this cheese. It has a much firmer texture than a fresh mozzarella and melts like a dream, but mozzarella will do nicely in its absence, in which case a bog-standard cow's milk variety will have a texture more in keeping with scamorza rather than one made with buffalo's milk. This omelette is very true to the diet with whole grains whisked into the egg, two veggies and nuts to boot.

1. Season the tomatoes with a little salt in a small bowl and set aside. Whisk the eggs with a little seasoning in a small bowl, then stir in the grains.

2. Preheat the grill to high. Preheat a 24cm (9½in) non-stick frying pan, with a heatproof handle, over a medium heat. Add 1 teaspoon of oil to the frying pan, stir in the garlic and add half the spinach and fry until it wilts, add the remaining spinach and fry until wilted. Transfer to a medium bowl.

3. Return the frying pan to the heat, add the remaining oil, then tip in the eggs and grains and evenly spread over the base of the pan. Cook for 1–2 minutes until sizzling around the edges and golden underneath. At the same time, scatter over the spinach and lay the cheese on top.

4. Pop under the grill for 2–3 minutes or until golden and sizzling. Stir the pine nuts into the tomatoes and serve this piled on top of the omelette.

SERVES 2

READY IN 25–35 MINUTES

VEGETARIAN

LEEK AND EMMENTAL SCRAMBLED EGGS

- 1 tbsp extra virgin olive oil
- 300g trimmed leeks, halved lengthways and thinly sliced
- 1 tsp fresh thyme leaves
- sea salt and freshly ground black pepper
- 2 large free-range eggs
- 50g Emmental, coarsely grated
- 1 tbsp toasted flaked almonds

This one is my idea of heaven and is wickedly unctuous. If you are cooking for children you can leave out the nuts and thyme. As with all scrambles, it is at its best with a slice of hot toast (wholegrain, naturally), lightly buttered or drizzled with oil.

1. Heat the oil in a large non-stick frying pan over a medium-low heat and fry the leeks with the thyme and some seasoning for about 10 minutes until silky, well-reduced and just starting to colour, stirring frequently. Leave to cool for at least 10 minutes.

2. Whisk the eggs in a large bowl, then stir in the cheese and fold in the leeks. Transfer the mixture to a small non-stick saucepan and gently scramble over a low heat until the cheese has melted and the eggs have thickened; they should be creamy without turning to curds.

3. Serve scattered with the almonds.

SERVES 4

READY IN 30–35 MINUTES

VEGETARIAN

EGG-FRIED SPELT

- 200g pearled spelt
- 2 large free-range eggs
- 1 tbsp toasted sesame oil
- sea salt and freshly ground black pepper
- 1 tbsp vegetable oil
- 4 spring onions, trimmed and finely sliced

Another big easy, and a favourite in our house: for lunch, splashed with soy sauce, no further ado. It's a good one for using up any leftover pre-cooked spelt in the fridge, in which case it makes for a whizzy fry-up, especially good with some sautéed mushrooms.

1. Bring a large pan of water to the boil, add the spelt and simmer for 20–25 minutes until tender, then drain into a sieve and leave for a few minutes to steam-dry (the spelt can also be precooked and used from cold).

2. Whisk the eggs with the sesame oil and some seasoning in a bowl.

3. Heat the vegetable oil in a large non-stick frying pan over a medium heat, add the eggs and then straightaway add the spelt and stir brusquely to coat it. Fry for 2–3 minutes, turning occasionally, then remove from the heat and stir in the spring onions.

SERVES 2

READY IN 30–35 MINUTES

VEGETARIAN

RANCHOS EGGS WITH CAULIFLOWER AND LENTILS

- 2 tbsp extra virgin olive oil
- 3 banana shallots, peeled, halved and thinly sliced across
- 300g large cherry tomatoes, quartered
- 1 heaped tsp harissa
- 1 tbsp sun-dried tomato paste
- sea salt
- 300g small cauliflower florets
- 100g cooked green lentils
- 2 large free-range eggs
- 60g Manchego, finely diced
- 2 tbsp coarsely chopped fresh coriander

For those who like to kickstart the weekend with something spicy this makes a lavish brunch dish or Friday-night lead-in. A wholegrain bread fits nicely here, and I don't bother to skin the tomatoes – it will be all the more wholesome.

1. Heat the olive oil in a 24cm (9½in) non-stick frying pan over a medium heat and fry the shallots for 6–8 minutes until golden, stirring frequently.

2. Add the tomatoes and stir for a few minutes until they turn mushy and partially collapse. Stir in the harissa, the sun-dried tomato paste and some salt. Stir in the cauliflower, cover the pan with a tight-fitting lid and cook over a low heat for 15 minutes until the cauliflower is tender, stirring halfway through. Stir in the lentils.

3. Make 2 craters in the mixture and break an egg into each one, then scatter over the cheese. Cover and cook for a further 4–5 minutes until the eggs are just set but the yolks remains runny.

4. Scatter over the coriander and serve straightaway.

SERVES 4

READY IN 25–30 MINUTES

VEGETARIAN

GRIDDLED BROCCOLI AND POACHED EGGS WITH PINE NUT BREADCRUMBS

- sea salt and freshly ground black pepper
- 400g Tenderstem broccoli, trimmed
- 4 tbsp extra virgin olive oil
- 50g fresh wholemeal breadcrumbs
- 50g pine nuts, chopped
- finely grated zest of 1 lemon (optional)
- slug of white wine vinegar or cider vinegar
- 4 large free-range eggs

I buy Tenderstem broccoli on pretty much every visit to the supermarket. It's delicious cold for dunking into any dip, and I eat the spears as an alternative to bread or crackers, from preference. This way of griddling it is one step on from boiling and is great for building into a salad.

1. Bring a large pan of salted water to the boil, add the broccoli and cook for 3 minutes, then drain into a colander and leave for a few minutes to steam-dry.

2. Heat a ridged griddle pan over a medium heat. Toss the broccoli in a large bowl with 2 tablespoons of oil and some seasoning and cook in two to three batches for 2–3 minutes on each side, until golden, turning it using tongs.

3. For the crumbs, heat the remaining oil in a large non-stick frying pan over a medium heat. Add the breadcrumbs and nuts and fry for about 5 minutes until golden and crisp, stirring almost constantly, adding the lemon zest towards the end, if including. Drain on a double thickness of kitchen towel and leave to cool for at least 10 minutes.

4. Meanwhile, poach the eggs according to the method on page 81 and serve on top of the broccoli, scattered with the crumbs. Season to taste.

SERVES 4

READY IN 25–30 MINUTES

PESCATARIAN

SALMON SALAD NIÇOISE

300g cherry tomatoes, halved or quartered
sea salt and freshly ground black pepper
350g skinless salmon fillets
4 large free-range eggs
70g fine green beans, trimmed and halved
80g rocket leaves
approximately 2 tbsp extra virgin olive oil
100g pitted green or black olives
lemon wedges to serve

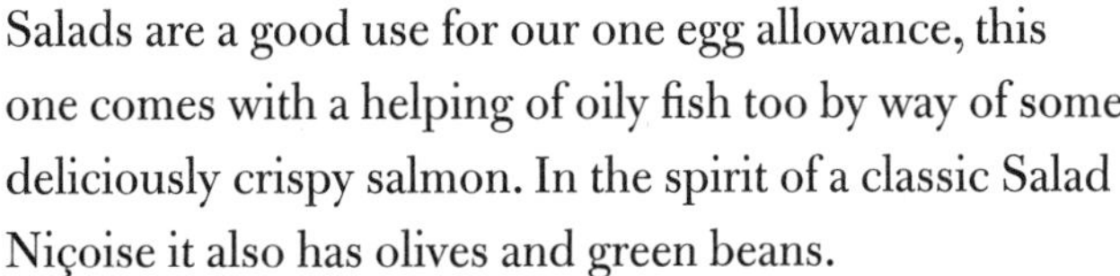

Salads are a good use for our one egg allowance, this one comes with a helping of oily fish too by way of some deliciously crispy salmon. In the spirit of a classic Salad Niçoise it also has olives and green beans.

1. Season the tomatoes with salt in a medium bowl and set aside.

2. Heat a large non-stick frying pan over a medium-high heat. Season the salmon fillets and depending on their thickness dry fry for 3–5 minutes on each side, until golden and crusty on the outside and just cooked through; there should be a slight give when you press them. Transfer these to a plate, leave to cool and then break into pieces.

3. Bring two medium pans of water to the boil. Add the eggs to one and cook for 8 minutes, then drain the pan, refill with cold water, leave them to cool and then shell and quarter. Add the beans to the other pan and cook for 3–4 minutes until just tender, then drain into a sieve and refresh under cold water.

4. Separately toss the rocket leaves and green beans with a little oil, then layer the ingredients on plates as follows: rocket, beans, salmon, tomatoes, with the eggs on top and around, and finally the olives. Accompany with lemon wedges.

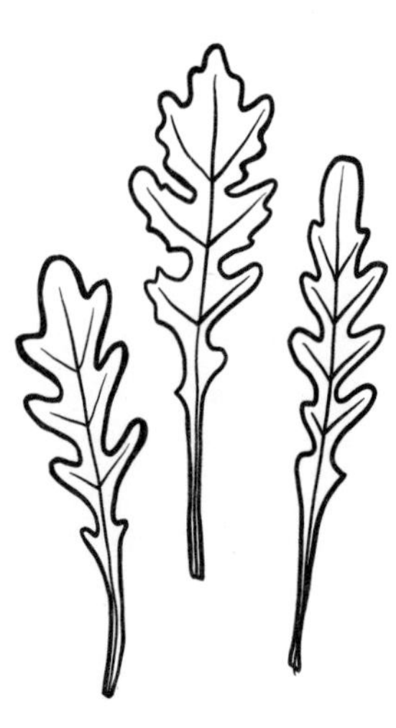

SERVES 4

READY IN 20 MINUTES

VEGETARIAN

CORN TORTILLAS WITH BROAD BEAN GUACAMOLE AND FRIED EGGS

100g frozen baby broad beans
3–4 tbsp extra virgin olive oil
sea salt
2 avocados, halved and pitted
1 tbsp lemon juice
1 tbsp coarsely chopped fresh flat-leaf parsley, plus a little extra to serve
4 large free-range eggs
4 corn tortillas or wholemeal flatbreads
Tabasco sauce to serve

This is a great inbetweeny snack – brunch, lunch, a light or pre-supper. Splash over a little of your favourite chilli sauce – a few drops of Tabasco are ideal. You could also serve these on pancakes (see page 75) instead of the tortillas.

1. Bring a small pan of water to the boil, add the broad beans and cook according to the packet instructions then drain into a sieve. Whizz to a coarse paste with 2 tablespoons of olive oil and a little salt in a food processor and leave to cool. Add the avocado flesh and the lemon juice and whizz again to a textured purée. Stir in the parsley.

2. Heat a medium non-stick frying pan over a medium heat, trickle 2 teaspoons of olive oil over the base, break in 2 eggs and fry for 2–3 minutes until lacy and crisp at the edges, basting the yolk with the hot fat until the white turns translucent. Transfer to a warm plate and cook the remaining eggs, adding a little more oil to the pan.

3. At the same time heat a second frying pan over a low heat and warm the tortillas or flatbreads on each side, one at a time. Arrange these on plates and spread the guacamole to within a couple of centimetres of the edge. Place a fried egg in the middle, scatter over a little more parsley and season with a drop or two of Tabasco.

SERVES 2

READY IN 15–20 MINUTES

VEGETARIAN

DEEP-FILLED MUSHROOM OMELETTE

approximately 3 tbsp extra virgin olive oil
1 banana shallot, peeled and finely chopped
400g mixed mushrooms, trimmed and torn or sliced as necessary
sea salt and freshly ground black pepper
squeeze of lemon juice
2 tbsp coarsely chopped fresh flat-leaf parsley
60g fresh goat's cheese, crumbled
2 large free-range eggs
25g roasted chopped hazelnuts, or sunflower seeds

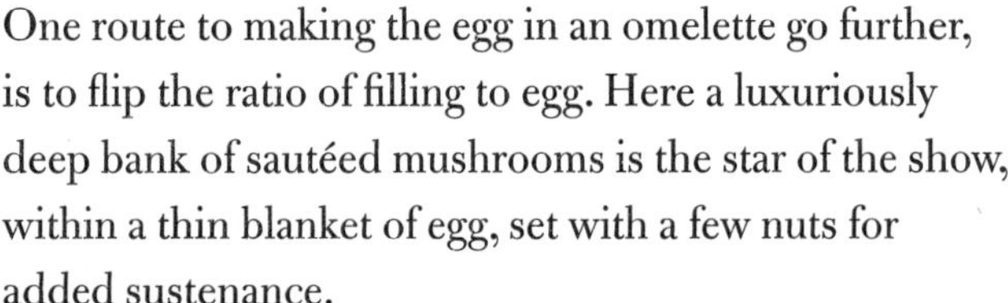

One route to making the egg in an omelette go further, is to flip the ratio of filling to egg. Here a luxuriously deep bank of sautéed mushrooms is the star of the show, within a thin blanket of egg, set with a few nuts for added sustenance.

1. Heat a medium non-stick frying pan over a medium-high heat, add 1 tablespoon of olive oil and half the shallot and cook briefly until translucent. Throw in half the mushrooms without overcrowding the pan, otherwise they will stew, and fry for a few minutes, stirring occasionally until golden. If any liquid is given out, continue to fry until they are dry and coloured. Remove to a warm bowl and cook the remaining mushrooms in the same way, then add these to the bowl. Season, add a squeeze of lemon, stir in the parsley and cheese.

2. Meanwhile, whisk the eggs in a small bowl, season and stir in the nuts.

3. Return the frying pan to the heat, drizzle a teaspoon of oil over the base, add the egg mixture and scramble with a fork until half set. Cook for a minute or two longer until the egg has nearly set, scattering the mushrooms over the top. Fold the omelette over and cook for about 30 seconds longer, then slip it onto a warm plate to serve.

SERVES 4

READY IN 15 MINUTES

VEGETARIAN

HALLOUMI PITTAS WITH POACHED EGGS

- slug of white wine vinegar or cider vinegar
- 4 large free-range eggs
- 300g fine asparagus spears, trimmed
- extra virgin olive oil for drizzling
- 2 wholemeal pittas
- 200g halloumi, cut into 1cm (½in) slices

Halloumi lends brio to a cheese-on-toast line-up, here with some asparagus spears and a poached egg. All manner of green veg will stand here – spinach, green beans, broccoli spears, also roast veg.

1. Poach the eggs according to the method on page 81, then transfer them to a bowl.

2. Meanwhile, arrange the asparagus tips in a steamer, insert over a medium saucepan with a little simmering water in it, cover and steam for 3 minutes. Transfer the asparagus to a bowl and toss with a little oil.

3. Toast the pittas and slit in half. For the cheese, heat a large non-stick frying pan over a medium heat and toast the slices for about 1 minute on each side until golden.

4. Scoop the cheese slices onto the warm halves of pitta bread, arrange the asparagus on top and then the eggs.

SERVES 4

READY IN 20–25 MINUTES

VEGETARIAN

TOASTED GOAT'S CHEESE WITH GARLIC SPINACH

500g spinach
approximately 3 tbsp extra virgin olive oil
1 garlic clove, peeled and crushed to a paste
sea salt and freshly ground black pepper
2 x approximately 150g medium-mature goat's cheeses, e.g. Kidderton Ash
1 tbsp fresh thyme leaves (optional)
slug of white wine vinegar or cider vinegar
4 large free-range eggs
squeeze of lemon juice
4 slices of wholegrain bread

Another route to cheese on toast is to bake the cheese in the oven and then dollop it onto crisp slices of toast. Goat's cheeses always bake to a divinely moussey melt. This is a little bit more cheese than the daily allowance (see page 16), so maybe give dairy a miss the day after.

1. Pass the spinach under a cold tap in a colander, then shake the leaves dry and place the spinach in a large saucepan, cramming the leaves down to get it all in. Cover with a tight-fitting lid and cook over a medium heat for 10–15 minutes or until the spinach has completely wilted, pressing it down halfway through.

2. Drain into a sieve and press out as much liquid as possible. Heat 2 tablespoons of oil in the saucepan with the garlic over a medium heat, until it sizzles and turns fragrant, then add the spinach and some seasoning and stir to coat.

3. Meanwhile, preheat the oven to 220°C (fan 200°C/gas mark 7). Place the goat's cheeses in a small baking dish, scatter over the thyme, if including, trickle a teaspoon of oil over each one and bake for 10 minutes until golden in patches. The cheese should retain its shape while being molten inside.

4. Meanwhile poach the eggs (see method on page 81).

5. Reheat the spinach over a medium heat and season with a squeeze of lemon.

6. Toast the bread and place on the table with the cheese, spinach and eggs to serve.

SERVES 2
(MAKES APPROXIMATELY 4)

READY IN 15 MINUTES

VEGETARIAN

SIMPLY PANCAKES

1 medium free-range egg
150ml skimmed milk
2 tsp vegetable oil
pinch of sea salt
60g wholemeal spelt flour

No introduction needed, which won't stop me waxing lyrical about their adaptability come breakfast or supper (see pages 76–77).

This is the same recipe that I use with plain white flour and 10g of unsalted butter in lieu of oil, but it's good to see how the pancakes can be tailored to improve their nutritional value and tick the Healthy Planet boxes.

For the batter

In a blender: Place the egg, milk, oil and salt in a blender, then add the flour and whizz until smooth. Scrape down any flour clinging to the sides and whizz again.

By hand: Whisk the egg in a small bowl, then stir in the flour, add the salt and mix to a lumpy dough. Gradually whisk in the milk until smooth and add the oil.

To cook the pancakes

Heat a 24cm (9½in) non-stick frying pan over a medium-high heat for several minutes. Ladle in just enough batter to coat the base, tipping it to allow it to run evenly over the surface. When the pan is hot enough, the pancake mixture should sizzle as it hits the pan, cook for 30 seconds until the top side appears dry and lacy at the edges and it is golden and lacy underneath. Loosen the edges using a palette knife or non-stick spatula, slip this

continued overleaf ▶

underneath and flip it over. Give it another 30 seconds and then slip it onto a plate. I always discard the first one; for no explicable reason it never seems to work properly.

GET AHEAD

You can also make these in advance, cover and chill the pancakes once they are cool, and reheat them briefly on each side in a dry frying pan. In this case they keep well for several days.

BREAKFAST PANCAKES

SERVES 2–4 (MAKES APPROXIMATELY 8)

READY IN 25 MINUTES

VEGETARIAN

2 x quantity of batter (see page 75) plus 1 heaped teaspoon of caster sugar

TOPPING SUGGESTIONS

berries and Greek yoghurt
apple purée and cinnamon
mashed banana and raisins

Pancake mornings are still a fixture in our house, despite my youngest son being twenty-two years old, there is nothing quite a like a stack of lacy pancakes building up on the table to bring out your inner child.

1. Cook the pancakes following the instructions on page 75.

2. You can either dish up the pancakes as they are cooked or pile them up on a plate and cover with foil to keep warm.

3. Serve with the toppings of your choice.

SERVES 2–4 (MAKES APPROXIMATELY 8)

READY IN 25 MINUTES

VEGETARIAN/PESCATARIAN

SUPPER PANCAKES

2 x quantity of batter (see page 75)

TOPPING SUGGESTIONS

fresh goat's cheese and roast red peppers
sautéed mushrooms and grated Emmental
smoked salmon and alphalfa

I also found as my children were growing up, pancakes were a great way of introducing a little independence at the table. By setting out an array of nutritious fillings, they were in charge.

1. Cook the pancakes following the instructions on page 75.

2. You can either dish up the pancakes as they are cooked or pile them up on a plate and cover with foil to keep warm.

3. Serve with the toppings of your choice.

SERVES 4
(MAKES APPROXIMATELY 12 SMALL PANCAKES)

READY IN 25–30 MINUTES

FLEXITARIAN

SPINACH AND PARMESAN PANCAKES

300–350g spinach
1 x quantity of batter (see page 75)
50g grated Parmesan, plus extra to serve
freshly grated nutmeg
sea salt and freshly ground black pepper
approximately 1 tbsp rapeseed oil

One step on from simply pancakes, these are gorgeously creamy and tender. Spinach with Parmesan belongs in the melt's hall of fame.

1. Pass the spinach under a cold tap in a colander. Place the spinach in a large saucepan, cover and cook over a low heat for 10–15 minutes or until it has wilted, stirring halfway through. Drain into the colander and press out the excess liquid as thoroughly as possible, then coarsely chop on a board.

2. Combine the spinach with the batter in a large bowl, then stir in the Parmesan and season with nutmeg, salt and pepper.

3. Heat a large non-stick frying pan over a medium heat, add a teaspoon of oil and drop in rounded tablespoons of the mixture, spreading them out evenly into thick pancakes about 8cm (3¼in) in size, and fry for about 1 minute on the first side and 30–60 seconds on the second side. Drain them on a double thickness of kitchen towel and cook the remainder, adding a drop more oil to the pan if necessary.

4. Serve the pancakes dusted with a little extra Parmesan.

SERVES 4

READY IN 15 MINUTES

VEGETARIAN

SPICY OMELETTE STRIPS

4 large free-range eggs
1 tbsp lemon juice
3 heaped tbsp coarsely chopped fresh coriander
sea salt
2 tbsp vegetable oil
1 tsp finely chopped fresh root ginger
1 garlic clove, peeled and finely chopped
1 heaped tsp finely chopped medium-hot green chilli

These delicate omelette strips, fired up with ginger, garlic and chilli, are an excellent use for our weekly egg, that will accessorize any number of dishes, as suggested on page 80. Or just use them to accompany whatever grazing goodies you have in the fridge – light supper sorted.

1. Whisk the eggs, lemon juice, coriander and a little salt in a medium bowl.

2. Heat 1 tablespoon of oil in a small saucepan over a medium heat and fry the ginger, garlic and chilli until the garlic just starts to colour, then whisk this into the eggs.

3. Fry the egg mixture, a third at a time, in a 24cm (9½in) non-stick frying pan over a medium heat, as though making pancakes, initially brushing the pan with vegetable oil. Cook the omelettes for about 1 minute or until dry on the surface, then turn using a spatula and cook for another 30–45 seconds. Cut them into broad strips 3–4cm (1¼–1½in) wide, and then halve. Serve hot or warm.

continued overleaf ▶

TIPS FOR THE TABLE

Use these to fill warm wholemeal pitta breads, with sliced cherry tomatoes and spring onions, shredded lettuce and a cucumber raita.

Scatter these over Coconut dal curry (see page 107).

Serve these scattered over a curried vegetable soup such as butternut, spinach or mushroom.

Make these part of a platter, with a lentil salad, a beetroot salad, griddled Tenderstem broccoli (see page 69) and roasted almonds.

POACHED AND FRIED EGGS

A single poached or fried egg rounds off any number of dishes in way that turns them into a main (see my Tips for the table, page 83). It's that little bit of extra protein that leads to a sense of satiety, and they are ever luxurious with a runny yolk.

POACHED EGGS

READY IN 10 MINUTES

VEGETARIAN

slug of white wine vinegar or cider vinegar
large free-range egg(s)

I far prefer free-form, splodgy poached eggs achieved by a few minutes in a hot water bath – a saucepan of almost simmering water – to the neat package of an egg cooked in a poaching pan. So here's how. The aim is for a lightly poached egg with an opaque casing of white enclosing a golden river of liquid yolk within, one of the master strokes of luxury.

1. Fill a large saucepan with water if you are cooking several eggs, a smaller one if it is just one or two, and bring it to the boil. Add a good slug of white wine vinegar or cider vinegar. Now turn the heat down and keep the water at a trembling simmer, it mustn't boil while the egg(s) are poaching.

2. Break the egg(s), one at a time, into a cup. Gently stir the water into a whirlpool using a large spoon and drop the egg(s) into it. They will immediately sink to the bottom of the pan leaving strands of white floating. After about

continued overleaf ▶

2 minutes they will rise to the surface. Cook them for 2 minutes longer and then remove them using a slotted spoon, trimming off the tendrils of white against the side of the saucepan.

FRIED EGGS

READY IN 5 MINUTES

VEGETARIAN

2 tsp groundnut or vegetable oil
large free-range egg(s)
sea salt and freshly ground black pepper

Fried eggs are where we get fussy, there is the potential for an infinite number of ways of how you like them cooked. For me personally, as I have an aversion to wobbly egg white, I like mine fried to a crisp on the base and around the edges, and flipped at the last minute to set the top. You can cook up to a couple of eggs in a frying pan in one go. A non-stick pan ensures they glide with ease out of the pan and you don't risk tearing the yolk.

1. Heat a large non-stick frying pan over a medium-high heat and then trickle the oil over the base. Break in the egg(s), season with sea salt and black pepper and fry for about 2 minutes until golden on the underside. The edges should look lacy and crisp. If you are cooking two, and the white joins together then separate them with a spatula.

2. Very carefully turn and cook the yolk side for about 10 seconds to just set the surface, then slip out of the pan onto a plate, turning the egg(s) the right way up.

TIPS FOR THE TABLE

Serve on top of a pile of buttered asparagus or griddled Tenderstem broccoli with a dusting of Parmesan.

Drop into a bowl of vegetable soup.

Serve on top of a leafy salad with some green beans and peas.

Serve on a pile of spicy baked beans or other pulses, such as the Garlicky white beans with spinach (see page 110).

Serve with a vegetable ragout such as ratatouille or piperade.

Serve with a mushroom fry-up with some added chickpeas or cannellini beans.

Pop on top of a pile of roast vegetables on wholegrain toast.

Serve on top of a simple wholegrain pilaf with added veggies.

COMFORTING STEWS AND CURRIES

STEWS, CURRIES AND TAGINES ARE NATURAL VEHICLES FOR slender quantities of animal protein, be it those red meat special occasions, poultry or fish. Such dishes are as much about the sauce as the few treasured morsels within it, which will seep their savoury juices into the liquid as it simmers. The result is a wealth of flavour for very little outlay. Traditionally, such dishes were a way of making a little go a long way, so there is no sense of being short-changed with such dishes, in the way that you might if you were only allowed one slice of roast chicken or beef.

Their second great selling point is the natural side of a pilaf or pile of grains of some description, which is their ideal dancing partner; enter whole grains in their near infinite variety. You could cook up a pilaf, flavoured with spices, or leave it at a pile of very simply boiled spelt, freekeh, buckwheat or another personal favourite, wheat berries. There is enough going on in the sauce to compensate for such basics. Personally I like to cut grain sides half and half with another vegetable, or stir them through a pile of green leaves such as spinach or lamb's lettuce (I have a light appetite and am more inclined to eat ten different vegetables a day than piles of whole grains). But for the generous of appetite, these stews are a godsend, with the potential to leave you feeling well and truly sated.

Even though the drive behind this book is to inspire ways of how we can continue to eat animal proteins in the reduced quantities necessary to support environmental sustainability, there are any number of gorgeous vegan stews, tagines and curries that will nudge us in the direction of eating more plant foods. Lentils make for fabulous dals, although here I would be inclined to serve them with plenty of veggies or crisp, dark green leaves, and a bread, to balance out their character. The chapter Beyond potatoes (see page 147) is designed to go hand in hand with this chapter, with lots of ideas for light sides, so you can take any stew and dress it up to maximal nutritional benefit.

SERVES 6

READY IN 2 HOURS

FLEXITARIAN

LAMB, DATE AND TOMATO TAGINE

- 2 medium white or yellow onions, peeled and grated or finely chopped in a food processor
- 1 rounded tbsp ras-el-hanout or other tagine spice blend
- 500g leg of lamb, trimmed of fat, cut into 3–4cm (1¼–1½ in) dice
- juice of ½ lemon
- 250–300g plum or standard tomatoes, skinned and chopped
- 75g stoned Medjool dates, halved lengthways
- 4 tbsp coarsely chopped fresh coriander, plus extra to serve
- knob of unsalted butter
- sea salt
- 1 x 400g tin chickpeas, drained and rinsed
- 150g baby spinach leaves
- sesame seeds for sprinkling

Tagines, that often combine pulses with meat, are an excellent way of enjoying just a small amount. This one is born of the memory of watching stall holders preparing their lunchtime tagines at daybreak beside a mountain road in Ouarzazate, in Morocco, a testament to its simplicity. No fiddly sautéing of ingredients; instead time, a gentle heat and spices are its bedrock. Try serving with Spicy cauli with turmeric yoghurt (see page 136) and Bulgur wheat pilaf (see page 150).

1. Combine the onions and spice blend in a medium flameproof casserole dish. Add the lamb, lemon juice, tomatoes, dates, coriander, butter and 500ml water. Stir and season with salt, bring to the boil and skim off the surface foam, then cover and cook over a very low heat for 1½ hours.

2. Stir in the chickpeas. Scatter over the spinach, cover and cook for another 5 minutes, stirring the leaves into the tagine halfway through. Taste for seasoning and serve scattered with more coriander and sesame seeds.

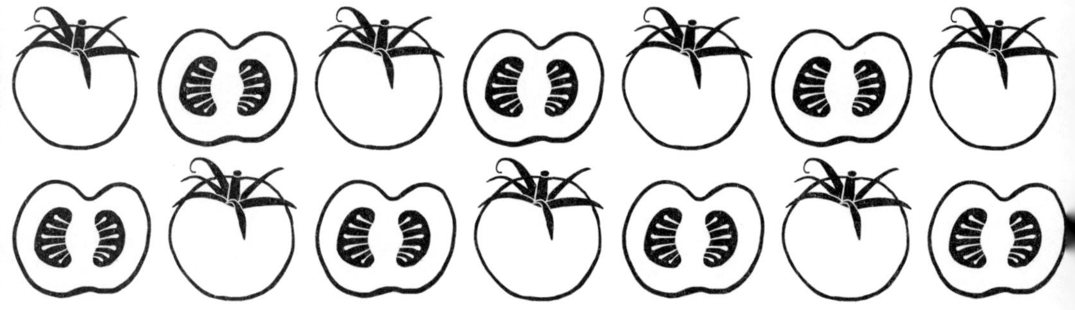

SERVES 6

READY IN 25 MINUTES

FLEXITARIAN

THAI CHICKEN AND EDAMAME BEAN CURRY

- 1 tbsp groundnut or vegetable oil
- 4 banana shallots, peeled and sliced
- 2 garlic cloves, peeled and sliced
- 2 level tbsp Thai green curry paste
- 425ml chicken stock
- 2 x 400ml tins full-fat coconut milk
- 6 lime leaves
- 4 medium-hot red chillies
- 500g cooked free-range chicken or turkey (white and dark meat), cut into 2–3cm (¾–1¼in) dice
- 200g frozen soya (edamame) beans
- 3 tbsp fish sauce
- 1 rounded tbsp caster sugar
- 20g fresh basil leaves
- 20g fresh coriander leaves, plus extra chopped to serve

Frozen soya beans, aka edamame beans, are one of my freezer staples. They are a rich source of plant protein that is at the ready to balance out dishes such as this, which have just a small amount of chicken or turkey. I normally take the easy route with this curry and buy the best ready-made curry paste I can find rather than starting from scratch. Instead of white rice, try serving this with the Lemon and pine nut brown rice pilaf (see page 152) or with some buckwheat noodles.

1. Heat the oil in a large flameproof casserole dish or saucepan over a medium-low heat and fry the shallots and garlic for a few minutes until they soften.

2. Stir in the curry paste and cook for a minute longer, then add the chicken stock, one of the tins of coconut milk, the lime leaves and the whole chillies. Bring this to the boil over a high heat, then simmer over a low heat for 10 minutes. You can prepare the recipe to this point in advance and finish cooking it 10 minutes before you want to eat.

3. Bring the sauce back to the boil over a medium heat, add the chicken or turkey and beans, then once it comes back to the boil simmer for 5 minutes. Stir the remaining can of coconut milk, the fish sauce, the sugar and the herbs into the curry, and bring back to the boil.

continued overleaf ▶

4. Serve the curry in shallow bowls, with some rice or noodles spooned to the side, and scatter over a little more coriander. You can leave in the whole chillies and lime leaves and remove them as you are eating.

VEGAN SWAP

Replace the chicken with thin strips of firm tofu, the edamame beans with peas (to maintain a balanced meal, as both tofu and edamame are soya), the chicken stock with vegetable stock, and the fish sauce with light soy sauce.

SERVES 6

READY IN
1 HOUR 30 MINUTES–
1 HOUR 40 MINUTES

FLEXITARIAN

HEALTHY PLANET CHILLI CON CARNE

2 tbsp extra virgin olive oil
1 medium white or yellow onion, peeled and finely chopped
2 slim carrots, trimmed, peeled, halved lengthways and thinly sliced
1 celery stick, trimmed, halved lengthways and thinly sliced
3 garlic cloves, peeled and finely chopped
½ tsp cayenne pepper
1 tsp ground cumin
400g minced beef
150g Puy lentils
150ml red wine
2 x 400g tins chopped tomatoes
2 tbsp tomato purée
1 small dried red chilli, crumbled
1 bay leaf
1 x 200g tin chickpeas or butter beans, drained and rinsed
sea salt

This ragù contains half the amount of beef as usual, bolstered with lentils that are so similar in texture and size that it is deceptively meaty. I like this every bit as much as, if not more than, a ragù made with pure beef.

1. Heat the olive oil in a medium-large saucepan over a medium heat, and fry the onion, carrot and celery for 7–10 minutes until softened and glossy, stirring frequently and adding the garlic and spices just before the end.

2. Add the minced beef, turn the heat up and fry, stirring frequently, until it changes colour.

3. Add the lentils, wine, 400ml water, tomatoes, purée, chilli and bay leaf. Bring to the boil, then simmer over a low heat for 1 hour, stirring now and again.

4. Stir in the pulses and simmer for another 10–20 minutes until firm. Season with salt.

continued overleaf ▶

VARIATION

VEGAN CHILLI

SERVES 6

READY IN 35–40 MINUTES

VEGAN

- 5 tbsp extra virgin olive oil
- 1 medium white or yellow onion, peeled and finely chopped
- 1 celery stick, trimmed, halved lengthways and thinly sliced
- 2 red peppers, core and seeds removed, and cut into 1–2cm (½–¾in) dice
- 3 garlic cloves, peeled and finely chopped
- 1 heaped tsp finely chopped medium-hot fresh red chilli
- ½ tsp cayenne pepper
- 1 heaped tsp ground cumin
- 1 level tsp ground cinnamon
- 1 heaped tsp dried oregano
- 1 bay leaf
- 2 x 400g tins chopped tomatoes
- 150ml vegan red wine
- sea salt and freshly ground black pepper
- 150g Puy lentils
- 400g mushrooms, stalks trimmed, halved and thinly sliced
- 400g aubergine, cut into 1cm (½in) dice

Vegans are well served here with a chilli made with mushrooms, aubergines and lentils, which is every bit as savoury as a chilli made with beef.

1. For the vegetable base, heat 1 tablespoon of olive oil in a medium-large saucepan over a medium heat and fry the onion and celery for 4–5 minutes until starting to colour, stirring frequently.

2. Add the red pepper and continue to fry for another 4–5 minutes until softened and lightly coloured, adding the garlic and chilli halfway through.

3. Stir in the spices and bay leaf, and add the tinned tomatoes, the wine and some seasoning. Simmer the sauce over a low heat for 15 minutes.

4. At the same time, bring a medium pan of water to the boil, add the lentils and simmer for about 20 minutes or until just tender, then drain them into a sieve.

5. While the sauce and lentils are cooking, heat 1 tablespoon of oil in a large non-stick frying pan over a medium-high heat and fry half the mushrooms for about 5 minutes until golden, stirring frequently and seasoning them towards the end. Transfer these to a bowl and repeat with the remaining mushrooms, then cook the aubergine in the same way.

6. Stir the vegetables and lentils into the base, bring to a simmer, cover and cook for 5 minutes.

TIPS FOR THE TABLE

A good chilli, like dal, can be dished up in endless ways, and always makes for great entertaining.

Serve with warmed tacos shells, guacamole, very finely sliced Romaine or Little Gem hearts, soured cream or crumbled feta (or vegan coconut yoghurt) and chopped coriander.

Serve with the Bulgur wheat pilaf (see page 150) or the Lemon and pine nut brown rice pilaf (see page 152), soured cream (or vegan coconut yoghurt), chopped coriander, sliced spring onions and lime wedges.

SERVES 6

READY IN 2 HOURS 30 MINUTES

FLEXITARIAN

BEEF HOTPOT WITH OLIVES AND PICKLED LEMON

- 3–4 tbsp extra virgin olive oil
- 600g stewing beef, cut into 3–4cm (1¼–1½in) dice
- sea salt and freshly ground black pepper
- 2 medium white or yellow onions, peeled, halved and thinly sliced
- 3 garlic cloves, peeled and crushed to a paste
- 1 tsp ground cumin
- ¼ tsp ground allspice
- pinch of dried chilli flakes
- 600g baby spinach leaves
- 150g pitted green olives
- squeeze of lemon juice

TO SERVE

- 3 baby pickled lemons, finely sliced and seeds removed
- 2 handfuls of fresh coriander leaves

Full of deep, rich flavours, lots of inky green spinach and tender morsels of braised beef in a dark gravy. This would go especially well with the Bulgur wheat pilaf (see page 150) or plain wholewheat couscous.

1. Heat 2 tablespoons of oil in large flameproof casserole dish over a high heat, add the meat, season and sear to colour all over. If necessary, do this in two batches to avoid overcrowding the dish.

2. Turn the heat down to medium, add the onion and fry for 5–7 minutes until coloured, stirring occasionally.

3. Stir in the garlic and spices, then add the meat back to the pan with 600ml water and some salt. Bring to the boil, cover and cook over a low heat for 2 hours until the meat is tender.

4. Towards the end of this time cook the spinach – you will need to do this in three or four batches. Heat a teaspoon of oil in a large non-stick frying pan over a high heat, add a pile of spinach and stir-fry until it wilts. Transfer to a bowl and repeat with the remainder.

5. Stir the spinach and olives into the stew base and heat through, and season with a squeeze of lemon juice.

6. Combine the pickled lemon and coriander in a bowl and serve as a little relish on top of the stew.

SERVES 6

READY IN 1 HOUR 40 MINUTES

FLEXITARIAN

CHICKEN AND BROAD BEAN STEW WITH POMEGRANATE

FOR THE CHICKEN

2 tbsp extra virgin olive oil
sea salt and freshly ground black pepper
6 skin-on free-range chicken pieces, e.g. thighs (bone-in) and drumsticks
1 medium white or yellow onion, peeled and halved
1 bay leaf
1 cinnamon stick

FOR THE STEW

2 tbsp extra virgin olive oil
3 white or yellow onions, peeled and chopped
2 celery sticks, trimmed and sliced
4 garlic cloves, peeled and finely chopped
400g trimmed leeks, sliced
½ tsp ground ginger
¼ tsp ground allspice
500g cooked baby broad beans
400g small turnips, peeled and cut into thin wedges or diced
several large handfuls of chopped fresh coriander
several large handfuls of chopped fresh dill
juice of ½–1 lemon
seeds of 1 pomegranate

This is a topsy-turvy stew, where first you poach the chicken, which creates a stock and a few morsels of meat. You then lightly cook the vegetables in the stock and throw in lots of herbs at the end. I like to use cooked broad beans here – I normally use frozen baby broad beans and cook them according to the packet instructions. If using fresh ones, then simmer for about 7 minutes or until tender. This would be good with a fluffy mound of buckwheat, roasted or unroasted.

1. Heat 2 tablespoons of oil in a large flameproof casserole dish over a high heat, season and colour the chicken pieces on all sides. Spoon off the excess fat, add 600ml water, the halved onion, bay leaf and cinnamon stick. Don't worry if the chicken isn't completely covered. Bring to the boil, then cover and cook over a low heat for 1 hour until the chicken is tender. Remove it, and strain and reserve the liquor.

2. Heat 2 tablespoons of oil in the cleaned-out casserole dish over a medium heat. Add the chopped onion and celery and fry for several minutes until softened, stirring occasionally, then add the garlic and leeks and cook for a couple of minutes longer.

3. Stir in the ginger and allspice, add the broad beans and turnips, and the chicken poaching liquor and some seasoning. Bring to the boil, cover and simmer for 15 minutes.

continued overleaf ▶

4. In the meantime, shred the chicken flesh, discarding the skin and bones. Add the chicken to the dish and heat through. Stir in the herbs and lemon juice, taste for seasoning and serve scattered with pomegranate seeds.

SPICY LEBANESE LAMB STEW

SERVES 6

READY IN 1 HOUR 30 MINUTES

FLEXITARIAN

- 4 tbsp extra virgin olive oil
- 3 medium white or yellow onions, peeled and chopped
- 6 garlic cloves, peeled and finely chopped
- ½ tsp ground cumin
- ½ tsp ground cinnamon
- 400g minced lamb
- 1 x 400g tin chopped tomatoes
- 1 tbsp tomato purée
- sea salt and freshly ground black pepper
- 75g pistachios
- 1 heaped tsp finely sliced medium-hot red chilli
- 500g green beans, trimmed and halved
- 200g feta, cut into 1–2cm (½–¾in) dice
- 2 handfuls of coarsely chopped fresh mint

Made using minced lamb, this will please lovers of a good shepherd's pie. Less the potato top, it is finished instead with some toasted feta and mint. It's a really easy basic that can be knocked up for supper with the minimum of fuss. It is also juicier than the norm and a good one for ladling over any wholegrain pilaf.

1. Heat 2 tablespoons of oil in a large flameproof casserole dish over a medium-high heat. Add the onion and fry for 7–10 minutes until golden, stirring occasionally and adding the garlic a minute or two before the end.

2. Stir in the spices, then add the mince and continue to fry until it changes colour. Add the tomatoes, tomato purée, 400ml water and plenty of seasoning. Bring to the boil, then cover and cook over a low heat for 45 minutes.

3. Stir in the pistachios, chilli and green beans, cover and cook for another 15–20 minutes or until the beans are tender, stirring halfway through.

4. Preheat the grill to high. Toss the feta and mint with a couple of tablespoons of oil in a bowl, scatter this over the stew and pop the casserole dish under the grill until the cheese is golden. Serve straightaway.

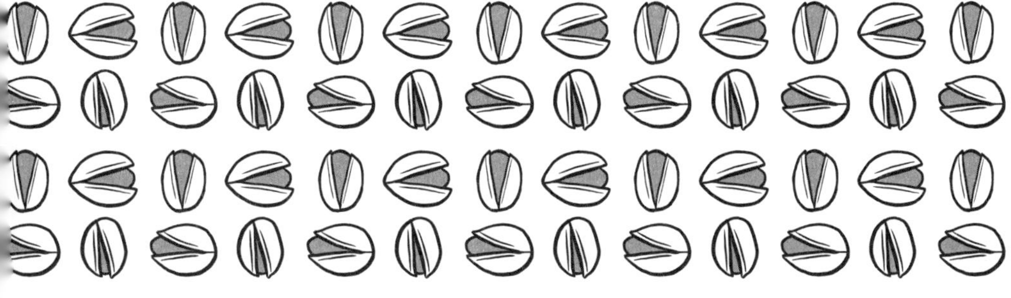

SERVES 4

READY IN 30 MINUTES

VEGETARIAN

GREEN VEGETABLE MINESTRONE WITH MINT AND ALMOND PESTO

8 tbsp extra virgin olive oil, plus extra for drizzling
1 celery heart, trimmed and sliced
2 leeks, trimmed and sliced
2 garlic cloves, peeled and finely chopped
150g French beans, ends trimmed and cut into 1cm (½in) pieces
150g fresh or frozen baby broad beans
150g fresh or frozen peas
800ml vegetable stock
sea salt and freshly ground black pepper
several handfuls of spinach leaves
25g fresh mint leaves
25g fresh flat-leaf parsley leaves
25g flaked almonds
75g grated vegetarian Parmesan-style cheese

A gorgeously thick, textured soup, a mass of lovely late spring veggies, you can include pretty much what you want here, so long as it's green.

1. Heat 3 tablespoons of oil in a large saucepan over a medium-low heat, add the celery and leeks and fry for 6–8 minutes until glossy and softened, stirring occasionally, adding the garlic just before the end.

2. Stir in the beans and peas, add the stock and season. Bring to the boil and simmer for 5 minutes. Add the spinach and cook for a minute longer.

3. Whizz half the soup in a food processor to a textured purée, then stir this back in with the rest of the soup.

4. Whizz the mint, parsley and almonds with 5 tablespoons of oil in a food processor, then add the cheese and briefly whizz again. Stir into the hot soup and serve with a drizzle of oil.

SERVES 4–6

READY IN 3 HOURS 15 MINUTES

VEGAN

RED PEPPER CONFIT

- **6 red peppers, core and seeds discarded, cut into thin strips (less than 1cm/½in) downwards**
- **3 medium white or yellow onions, peeled, halved downwards and thinly sliced into half moons**
- **1 heaped tsp finely chopped medium-hot red chilli**
- **3 tbsp extra virgin olive oil**
- **1 tbsp balsamic vinegar, plus 1 tsp**
- **1 tbsp lemon juice**
- **sea salt**

This sweet and silky red pepper compote is a great all-round basic, the starting point for any number of dishes, from a vegan stew to a light mezze or on-toast fare. Don't be put off by the cooking time, it takes all of 10 minutes to throw together.

1. Heat the oven to 150°C (fan 130°C/gas mark 2). Combine the peppers, onions and chilli in a large flameproof casserole dish, drizzle over the oil, 1 tbsp vinegar and lemon juice, season with salt and toss to coat. Cover and bake for 3 hours, stirring every hour, until the peppers and onions are soft, silky and sitting in a pool of juices.

2. Simmer over a medium heat on the hob for 5–10 minutes until the juices are thick and syrupy, stirring frequently to ensure the compote doesn't stick.

3. Stir in another teaspoon of vinegar and taste for seasoning. Serve hot or cold.

SERVING SUGGESTIONS

Stir in olives, capers, chopped parsley or torn basil, or scatter with roasted nuts.

Spoon over roast aubergine.

Serve with a poached or fried egg.

Add cooked green lentils or pulses for a vegan casserole.

Serve as a pasta sauce, scattered with grated cheese.

Serve on toast with Manchego or crumbled goat's cheese.

SERVES 6

READY IN 1 HOUR 45 MINUTES

FLEXITARIAN

LAMB AND BUTTERNUT STEW WITH PINE NUTS

- 7 tbsp extra virgin olive oil
- 600g leg of lamb, trimmed of fat and cut into 3–4cm (1¼–1½ in) dice
- sea salt and freshly ground black pepper
- 3 medium white or yellow onions, peeled, halved and sliced
- 10 garlic cloves, peeled and thinly sliced
- ½ tsp ground allspice
- ½ tsp ground cinnamon
- 1 x 400g tin chopped tomatoes
- 1 x butternut squash (approximately 900g)
- 30g pine nuts
- 30g coarsely chopped fresh flat-leaf parsley
- 30g coarsely chopped fresh coriander
- juice of ½ lemon

This spicy lamb stew is as much about the butternut squash as the meat, and is enlivened with large handfuls of fresh parsley and coriander at the end. Try scooping it up with warm wholegrain flatbreads.

1. Heat 2 tablespoons of oil in a large flameproof casserole dish over a high heat, add half the lamb, season and sear to colour it all over. Transfer this to a bowl and colour the remainder, adding a little more oil to the dish if necessary, then remove this also.

2. Turn the heat down to medium, add the onions and fry for 8–10 minutes until golden, stirring occasionally and adding the garlic a minute or two before the end.

3. Stir in the spices, then add the tomatoes. Return the lamb to the pan. Add 400ml water and some seasoning. Bring to the boil, cover and cook over a low heat for 1¼ hours or until the lamb is tender.

4. Meanwhile, peel the squash, quarter the bulb to remove the seeds and slice into wedges. Halve the remaining cylindrical trunk lengthways and cut into 1cm (½in) slices.

5. Towards the end of simmering the stew, heat 2 tablespoons of oil in a large non-stick frying pan over a medium-high heat. Add half the squash, season and colour it all over, then remove it and cook the remainder in the same fashion, again removing it at the end.

6. Add the pine nuts to the frying pan, and fry stirring constantly until golden, then remove.

7. Stir the squash into the stew, cover and cook for about 10 minutes or until it is tender.

8. Stir in the herbs and lemon juice, taste for seasoning and serve scattered with the pine nuts.

SERVES 4

READY IN 40–45 MINUTES

PESCATARIAN

CHILLI PRAWN AND CHICKPEA STEW

- 2 tbsp vegetable oil
- 3 banana shallots, peeled and finely chopped
- 1 tbsp finely chopped fresh root ginger
- 3 garlic cloves, peeled and finely chopped
- 1 x 400g tin chopped tomatoes
- ¼ tsp cayenne pepper
- sea salt
- 400g raw peeled king prawns
- 1 x 400g tin chickpeas, drained and rinsed
- 1 small handful of small fresh mint leaves
- ½ tbsp fine strips of medium-hot red chilli, approximately 5cm (2in) long

More in the way of bantering between seafood and pulses, this stew is only modestly juicy, which makes it perfect for scooping up with bread as well as spooning over noodles. Its flavour palette could be anywhere from Lebanon to Vietnam.

1. Preheat the oven to 220°C (fan 200°C/gas mark 7). Heat 1 tablespoon of oil in a medium saucepan over a medium heat and fry the shallot, ginger and garlic for a few minutes until softened, stirring frequently.

2. Add the tomatoes, cayenne and a little salt, bring to the boil and simmer over a low heat for about 20 minutes until you have a rich, well-reduced sauce. This can be made in advance and reheated.

3. Stir the prawns, chickpeas, half the mint leaves and the chilli strips into the sauce and transfer to a roasting tin or gratin dish that holds the stew in a shallow layer (approximately 20 x 30cm/8 x 12in).

4. Drizzle over 1 tablespoon of oil and roast for 12–14 minutes, then scatter over a few more mint leaves.

SERVES 4

READY IN 25–30 MINUTES

PESCATARIAN

SIMPLY SALMON AND PEA FISH STEW

- 2 tbsp extra virgin olive oil, plus extra for crostini
- 1 large white or yellow onion, peeled, quartered and thinly sliced
- 1 celery heart, trimmed and thinly sliced
- 4 garlic cloves, peeled and finely chopped, plus extra for crostini
- pinch of dried chilli flakes
- 1 bay leaf
- 150ml white wine
- 300ml fish or vegetable stock
- 200g fresh or frozen peas
- 200g baby plum or cherry tomatoes, halved
- 400g skinless salmon fillets, cut into 3–4cm (1¼–1½in) pieces
- sea salt and freshly ground black pepper

TO SERVE

- coarsely chopped fresh flat-leaf parsley
- toasted wholegrain baguette slices, rubbed with garlic and drizzled with oil

Fish stews tend to be such an event that a really down-to-earth and delicious one is a boon for any repertoire. The buttery texture of salmon with peas is one of the most comforting I can think of, and there's plenty of garlic and parsley, with crostini for soaking up the juices.

1. Heat the oil in a large saucepan over a medium heat, add the onion and celery and fry for 6–8 minutes until softened and translucent, stirring occasionally and adding the garlic halfway through.

2. Add the chilli and bay leaf, pour in the wine and simmer until well-reduced.

3. Add the stock and bring to a simmer, then stir in the peas and tomatoes, and bring back to the boil. Season the salmon with salt and pepper and stir into the stew, cover and cook gently for 3–4 minutes.

4. Taste for seasoning and serve scattered with parsley. Accompany with the toasts.

SERVES 4

READY IN 2 HOURS 45 MINUTES

VEGAN

SLOW-ROASTED TOMATO SAUCE AND ROAST TOMATOES

- 1.5kg medium tomatoes, quartered
- 1 tbsp fresh thyme leaves
- sea salt and freshly ground black pepper
- 1 tsp caster sugar
- 4 tbsp extra virgin olive oil

A couple of trays of slowly roasted tomatoes make for the double delight of a rich aromatic sauce, with extra roast tomatoes for scattering over. Serve the sauce and roast tomatoes with a pile of whole grains and a green salad, or with pasta (using one batch for 300g pasta – I like it tossed with wholegrain spelt penne, scattered with the roast tomatoes and drizzled with olive oil, and, if you're flexitarian, scattered with lots of Parmesan too). The tomatoes also make for a great fridge fallback, on toast with some olives, or with any relaxed spread of mezze.

1. Heat the oven to 140°C (fan 120°C/gas mark 1). Lay the tomato quarters out on a non-stick baking tray cut-side up, scatter over the thyme and season with salt and a sprinkling of sugar. Drizzle over the olive oil and bake them for 1 hour.

2. Scoop half of the tomatoes into a blender and return the remainder to the oven for another 1½ hours until they are half-cooked, resembling semi-dried tomatoes. Thoroughly whizz the tomatoes in the blender to a sauce, then transfer to a small saucepan and taste for seasoning.

3. Serve the sauce spooned over grains or tossed with pasta, with the roast tomatoes on top .

TIP

Try serving the tomatoes with wholegrain bruschetta: give a slice of wholegrain toast a couple of swipes with a clove of garlic if wished, then drizzle with olive oil.

SERVES 4

READY IN 20–25 MINUTES

PESCATARIAN

HERBY SEAFOOD STEW

- 2 tbsp extra virgin olive oil, plus extra to serve
- 1 bunch of spring onions, trimmed and cut into 1cm (½in) slices
- 1 tsp finely chopped medium-hot green chilli
- 1 cucumber, peeled, halved and cut into 3mm (⅛in) slices
- 250g baby spinach leaves
- 30g fresh mint leaves, coarsely chopped
- 30g fresh coriander leaves, coarsely chopped, plus a little extra to serve
- 300ml fish stock
- sea salt and freshly ground black pepper
- 300g skinless basa fillets, cut into approximately 3cm (1¼in) pieces
- 100g cooked peeled king prawns
- 1 x 400g tin black beans, drained and rinsed
- 1 tbsp lime juice

The base of this stew cooks in less than five minutes, and that speed is mirrored in its freshness – it comes loaded with coriander and mint, and cucumber makes for the most delicate of vegetables when lightly cooked. Basa is an Asian catfish that makes an inexpensive alternative to white fish, such as cod, for stews and curries. But any meaty white fish can be used in its place.

1. Heat the oil in a large flameproof casserole dish over a medium heat, add the spring onion and chilli and fry for about 1 minute, stirring frequently until glossy, then add the cucumber and fry for 1–2 minutes longer, stirring occasionally until it starts to turn translucent.

2. Add the spinach in two goes, stirring until this wilts, then stir in the herbs.

3. Add the stock and some seasoning and bring to the boil, season and stir the basa into the soup, cover and cook for 4 minutes, gently folding in the prawns and beans halfway through.

4. Again, very gently, stir in the lime juice and check the seasoning, and serve drizzled with oil and a little more coriander scattered over.

SCALLOP TIKKA

SERVES 4

READY IN 20–25 MINUTES PLUS UP TO 2 HOURS MARINATING (OPTIONAL)

PESCATARIAN

FOR THE MARINADE

1 tbsp vegetable oil
1 banana shallot, peeled and finely chopped
2 garlic cloves, peeled and finely chopped
1 tsp finely chopped fresh root ginger
1 tsp finely chopped medium-hot red chilli
⅓ tsp ground turmeric
¼ tsp ground cinnamon
½ tsp ground fenugreek
100g low-fat plain yoghurt
½ tsp cornflour

FOR THE SCALLOPS

400g scallop meats, side gristle discarded
100g frozen petit pois
sea salt
1 tbsp vegetable oil

TO SERVE

2 spring onions, trimmed and finely sliced diagonally
1 small handful of fresh coriander leaves
lime wedges
warm wholemeal chapattis or naan breads

This takes inspiration from one of the most delicious things I have ever eaten, a warm scallop sandwich in the Outer Hebrides, grilled over a fire built in the shelter of rocks leading up from the beach. Prepared scallop meats make this the quickest of suppers, at most you might have to remove the small white gristle at the side. You could serve this with the Coconut dal curry (opposite).

1. Heat 1 tablespoon of vegetable oil in a small non-stick frying pan over a medium heat and fry the shallot, garlic, ginger and chilli for a couple of minutes until softened, stirring frequently, then stir in the spices and cook a little longer until fragrant.

2. Transfer this to a food processor and leave for a few minutes to cool down, then add the yoghurt and cornflour and whizz to a purée.

3. Transfer this to a bowl and stir in the scallops. You can leave them to marinate for up to a couple of hours, in which case cover and chill them.

4. Preheat the oven to 240°C (fan 220°C/gas mark 9). Stir the peas into the scallops and season with salt and spread over the base of a roasting tin. Drizzle over 1 tablespoon of oil and roast for 9–12 minutes until the scallops are just cooked through, they should feel firm with a slight give.

5. Combine the spring onions and coriander leaves in a bowl and serve scattered over the tikka, accompanied by lime wedges and warm breads.

COCONUT DAL CURRY

SERVES 4

READY IN 1 HOUR 25 MINUTES

VEGAN

200g yellow split peas
½ tsp ground cumin
½ tsp turmeric
1 x 400ml tin light coconut milk
2 medium-hot red chillies
2 medium-hot green chillies
sea salt
2 tbsp vegetable oil
1 heaped tsp black onion seeds
6 curry leaves
3 shallots, peeled, halved and thinly sliced
3 garlic cloves, peeled and finely sliced
2 tomatoes, core removed and finely chopped
lemon wedges

Dal is one of the most versatile vegan curries, ultimately soothing and nourishing. There are so many ways of dishing this one up, with some roast vegetables on top, with a pilaf (such as Bulgur wheat pilaf, page 150) and also a crisp green salad.

1. Rinse the split peas in a sieve under the cold tap, then place them in a medium saucepan (ideally non-stick), with the cumin, turmeric, coconut milk and 600ml water.

2. Bring to the boil, then cover with a lid, leaving a gap for the steam to escape, and simmer for 1 hour, stirring occasionally. Add the chillies and some salt, and up to another 200ml water if the dal seems overly thick, and simmer for another 15 minutes.

3. Towards the end of this time, heat the oil in a large non-stick frying pan over a medium heat, add the onion seeds and curry leaves and fry momentarily until these start to colour, then add the shallot and garlic and continue to cook for a couple of minutes until lightly golden, stirring frequently.

4. Add the tomatoes, season with salt and cook for another couple of minutes until they soften without collapsing.

5. Stir half the tomato mixture into the dal purée and serve with the rest of the tomato spooned on top, accompanied by lemon wedges.

continued overleaf ▶

VARIATION

PAN-FRIED MACKEREL

SERVES 4

READY IN 10 MINUTES

PESCATARIAN

2 tsp vegetable oil
4 x 90–100g mackerel fillets, skin scored diagonally at 3–4cm (1¼–1½in) intervals
sea salt and freshly ground black pepper

I love the combination of a mealy pulse purée such as this dal with oily fish, cooked to a crisp at the edges. Mackerel, like salmon, works a treat with spices; both fish are regulars on my table in any one week.

Heat 1 teaspoon of oil in a large non-stick frying pan over a medium heat, season the fillets with salt and pepper on each side. Fry 2 fillets, skin-side down for 3 minutes until you can see that the fish is almost cooked through, then flip them over and cook the flesh for 1 minute. Repeat to cook the remaining fillets and serve on top of the dal.

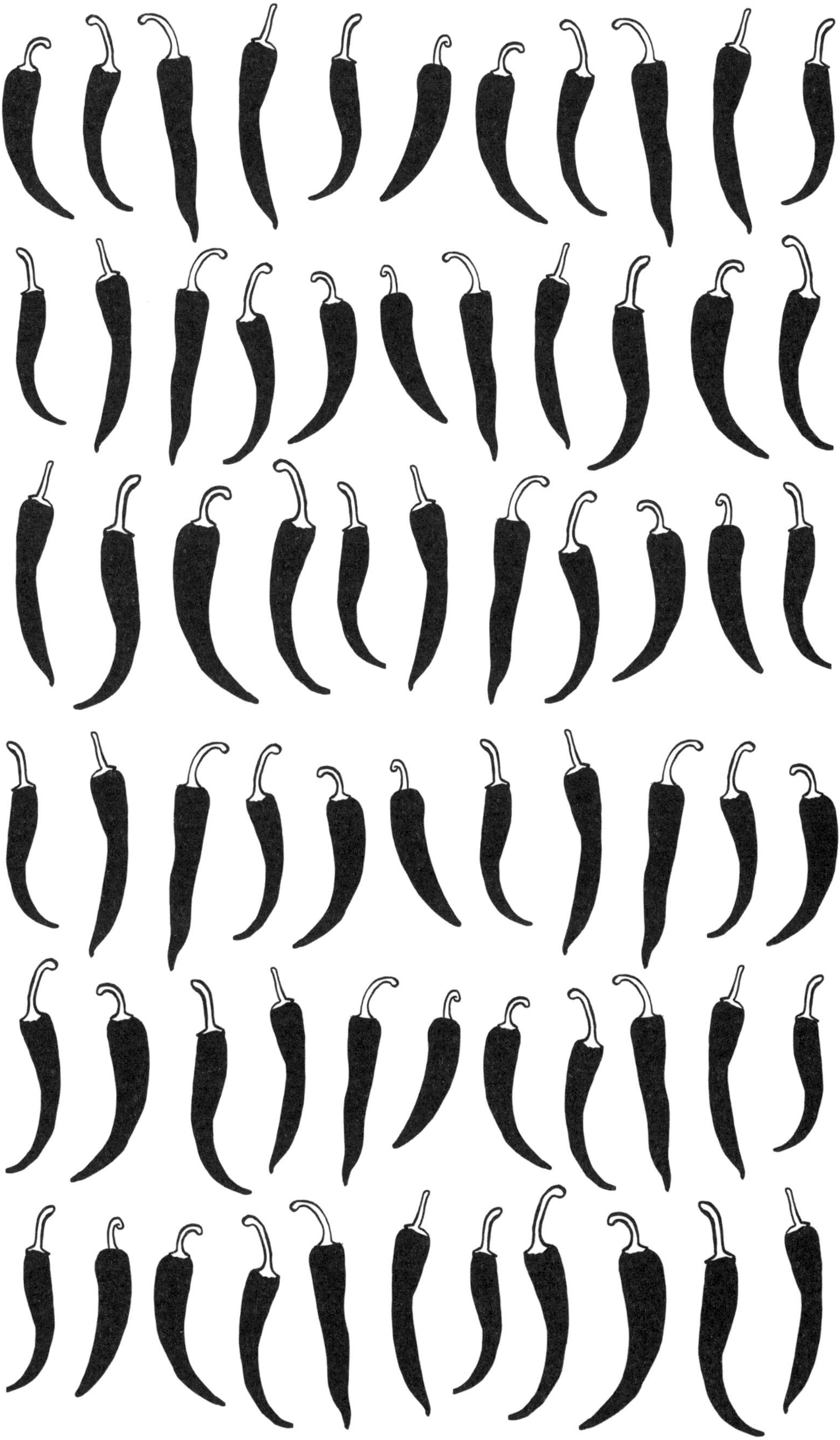

SERVES 4

READY IN 1 HOUR 45 MINUTES–2 HOURS, PLUS OVERNIGHT SOAKING

VEGAN

GARLICKY WHITE BEANS WITH SPINACH

300g dried haricot or cannellini beans
1 garlic head, papery outer skin removed and top cut off
2 bay leaves
2 tomatoes, halved
approximately 3 tbsp extra virgin olive oil, plus extra for drizzling
1 tbsp lemon juice, plus lemon wedges to serve
300g spinach
sea salt and freshly ground black pepper

Trapped at home during the lockdown I rediscovered the pleasures of slow-cooking. In particular soaking dried pulses overnight and then simmering them in the oven with a handful of aromatics.

Use this as a basic, for any dried pulse. They are especially good puréed with the garlic, with some beans left whole, but weave them into any number of dishes, such as salads, stir-fries or braised vegetable dishes like ratatouille, or stir into soups or stews at the end. They also provide the basis for a dip, or you could stir them into the tomato sauce on page 104 as a stew.

1. Place the beans in a large bowl, cover generously with cold water and set aside in a cool place to soak overnight.

2. Heat the oven to 160°C (140°C fan/gas mark 3). Drain the beans and place in a medium flameproof casserole dish, add 1.5 litres of water, bring to the boil and skim off the surface foam. Add the garlic, bay leaves and tomato and drizzle over 1 tablespoon of oil. Cover and cook in the oven for 1¼–1½ hours or until the beans are tender.

3. Reserve a splash of the cooking liquid and remove the aromatics. Drain the beans into a colander and place three quarters of these in a food processor. Squeeze out and add the inside of the garlic. Add the lemon juice, 1 tablespoon of oil and some seasoning and whizz to a creamy textured purée, adding a drop of the cooking liquid to achieve the right consistency. This can be made well in advance.

4. To serve, heat a large non-stick frying pan over a medium-high heat, add a trickle of oil and half the spinach and stir-fry until it wilts, then stir in half the reserved whole beans, season and heat through. Transfer to a bowl and repeat with the remaining spinach and beans.

5. If necessary, gently reheat the purée in a non-stick saucepan, stirring frequently. Spread over four warm dinner plates, scatter the spinach and beans on top, drizzle with extra oil and accompany with lemon wedges.

ALL-IN-ONE ROASTS AND PIES

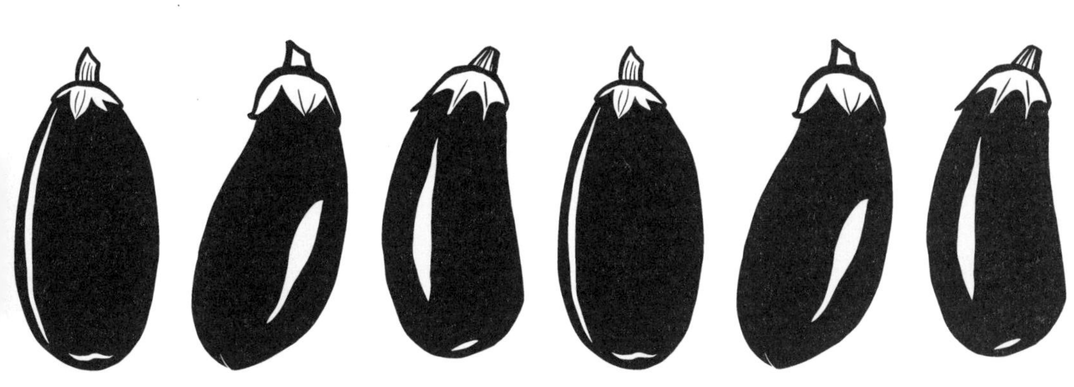

WHEN I FIRST READ THE RECOMMENDATIONS FOR HOW WE should eat and the considerable reduction in animal protein, my knee-jerk reaction was a widening of the eyes, and 'Oh no, but what about our lovely roasts?'. Unbearable. The thought that on future Sundays there would be no comforting golden chicken sizzling in a tray in the oven, crispy golden spuds below it, and a jug of gravy on the table. And what about a plate of thinly sliced roast beef with horseradish sauce, or belly of pork streaked with creamy layers of fat and a brittle shard of puffed-up crackling? I find it hard to contemplate life without them. And that is before we get to the comfort of pies – shepherd's pie, lasagne and steak pies – that up until now have been a given.

So, a large part of what I see as the challenge of this new way of eating, has been to find ways around how we can continue to have our roasts and our pies, without shouldering the guilt of ruining the planet's ecosystem with every bite, at which point they cease to taste as good as they used to. As with other chapters, it is about rethinking the originals, padding out much smaller quantities of animal protein with plant proteins. One of the win-wins of this approach is the penchant today for 'one tin' roasts, so everything sizzles together in a single pan, which makes for less washing-up, at the same time as getting a nutritious balance of protein and veg in there.

The second constraint on roasts and pies is the large amount of potatoes that so often go hand in hand, whether roast, chips or mash. So, partner this chapter with Beyond potatoes (see page 147), which seeks to replace them with identical foods, made using different vegetables. Sometimes, this rethink affords the advantage of dishes being altogether lower in carbs, which is great for our waistlines and supports a low-carb lifestyle, which is how I personally like to eat. So I am more than happy with a tray of roast celeriac wedges, courgette chips, honey and sesame roots as accompaniments to any of the dishes in this chapter.

SERVES 6

READY IN 2 HOURS

FLEXITARIAN

HEALTHY PLANET LASAGNE

FOR THE RAGÙ

2 tbsp extra virgin olive oil
2 leeks, trimmed, halved and sliced
3 red peppers, core and seeds removed, cut into 1–2cm (½–¾in) dice
3 garlic cloves, peeled and finely chopped
2 tsp rosemary needles, finely chopped
1 tsp fennel seeds, coarsely ground
½ tsp paprika
500g minced lamb
300ml red wine
1 x 540g jar passata
500ml lamb or chicken stock
sea salt and freshly ground black pepper
200g green lentils
200g cherry tomatoes, halved

continued opposite ▶

If you tease this recipe apart, it amounts to whole grains (the pasta), several different veggies (peppers, leeks, tomatoes), legumes (lentils), healthy fat (extra virgin olive oil), and just a little in the way of red meat that falls well within the recommended limit.

For a lasagne, this is light and juicy with a tomato base in lieu of a white sauce. In spirit it lies well south of Lyon. I'm happy to bask in the food of the Med all year round, but this is definitely one to graze on with a few salad leaves in the shade of a tree on a hot afternoon.

1. To make the ragù, heat the olive oil in a large saucepan over a medium heat and fry the leeks and red peppers for about 10 minutes until aromatic and lightly coloured, stirring in the garlic, rosemary, fennel and paprika a couple of minutes before the end.

2. Add the mince and cook, stirring frequently until it seals and changes colour. Pour in the red wine and simmer until reduced by half. Add the passata and stock, and season. Bring to a simmer and cook over a low heat for 45 minutes.

3. Meanwhile, bring a medium pan of water to the boil, add the lentils and simmer for 25 minutes or until just tender, then drain them into a sieve. Leave the sauce to stand for a few minutes, then skim off any oil on the surface and stir in the lentils; there should be lots of juices which will soak into the pasta as it bakes, keeping it really

FOR THE PASTA AND TOPPING

250–350g wholewheat lasagne
2 tbsp crème fraîche
60g grated Parmesan, plus extra to serve
100g baby peppers, core and seeds discarded and halved lengthways
1 tbsp extra virgin olive oil

succulent. Stir in the cherry tomatoes and check the seasoning.

4. Preheat the oven to 200°C (fan 180°C/gas mark 6). Select a 8 x 20 x 30cm (3¼ x 8 x 12in) roasting tin or baking dish (if your dish isn't quite deep enough, the lasagne won't come to any harm if you pile it a little higher than the top). Cover the base of the dish with a thin layer of ragù, then arrange a layer of lasagne on top, breaking the sheets to fit, and continue layering so you have about five layers of ragù in total and four of pasta, ending with ragù. Be sure to leave enough juices for this final layer so that it coats the pasta properly.

5. Dot the ragù with the crème fraîche, scatter over the Parmesan, then the baby peppers and finally drizzle over the oil. Bake for 35–40 minutes until golden and sizzling. You can also prepare the lasagne up to 12 hours before you need it, in which case leave the sauce to cool before assembling it, and then chill until required. It may take 5–10 minutes longer to cook. Serve with extra Parmesan.

continued overleaf ▶

VARIATION

TOMATO AND BASIL LASAGNE

SERVES 6

READY IN 1 HOUR 40 MINUTES

VEGETARIAN

FOR THE TOMATO SAUCE

1.3kg beefsteak tomatoes
3 tbsp extra virgin olive oil
1 medium white or yellow onion, peeled and finely chopped
4 garlic cloves, peeled and finely chopped
2 tbsp tomato purée
75ml vegetarian red wine
1 bay leaf
2 sprigs of fresh thyme
1 tsp caster sugar
sea salt and freshly ground black pepper

FOR THE PASTA AND TOPPING

230–350g wholewheat lasagne
3 buffalo mozzarella (350g), diced
75g grated vegetarian Parmesan-style cheese
8 large fresh basil leaves, torn in half
1 tbsp extra virgin olive oil

This vegetarian tomato and basil lasagne is delectably light and juicy.

1. To skin the tomatoes, bring a large pan of water to the boil. Cut out a cone from the top of each tomato to remove the core, plunge them into the boiling water for 20 seconds and then into a sink of cold water. Slip off the skins and coarsely chop them.

2. To cook the tomato sauce, heat the olive oil in a medium saucepan over a medium heat, add the onion and fry for a few minutes until soft and translucent. Add the garlic and stir it around, then add the tomatoes, the tomato purée, the wine, bay leaf and thyme. Bring to a simmer then cook over a low heat for 30 minutes, stirring occasionally.

3. Discard the herbs and beat the sauce to a slushy purée using a wooden spoon. Add the sugar and season with salt and pepper.

4. Preheat the oven to 200°C (fan 180°C/gas mark 6). Select a 8 x 20 x 30cm (3¼ x 8 x 12in) roasting tin or baking dish, cover the base with some of the tomato sauce, then layer the ingredients as follows. First a layer of lasagne, cover this with tomato sauce, scatter over some mozzarella and some of the Parmesan-style cheese and dot with a couple of the torn basil leaves. Continue layering with the remaining ingredients, ending with

tomato sauce and cheese, omitting the basil from this top layer. You should have four layers of pasta in all. Drizzle the olive oil over the surface and cover with foil. You can prepare the lasagne to this point in advance and chill it for up to 12 hours until you need it, in which case it may take 5–10 minutes longer to cook.

5. Bake the lasagne for 20 minutes, then remove the foil and bake for another 25 minutes until the top is golden and bubbling. If necessary, you can give it a few minutes under a grill, preheated to high, to brown. Serve straightaway.

SERVES 6

READY IN 1 HOUR 25 MINUTES

FLEXITARIAN

CRISPY-TOPPED SHEPHERD'S PIE

FOR THE FILLING

- **1 tbsp extra virgin olive oil**
- **3 banana shallots, peeled and finely chopped**
- **3 garlic cloves, peeled and finely chopped**
- **400g minced lamb**
- **1 tsp ground cumin**
- **1 tsp ground coriander**
- **1 small dried red chilli, crumbled**
- **150ml red wine**
- **200ml tomato passata**
- **sea salt**
- **300g frozen baby broad beans**
- **50g pine nuts**
- **75g pitted green olives, sliced**
- **30g fresh coriander, coarsely chopped**

FOR THE TOPPING

- **800g celeriac, skin cut off and cut into large chunks**
- **4 tbsp extra virgin olive oil**
- **sea salt and freshly ground black pepper**
- **1 bunch of spring onions, trimmed and sliced**
- **150g small cherry tomatoes, halved**

Like the Healthy Planet lasagne on page 116, take this apart and we have legumes (broad beans), several different veggies (shallots, tomatoes, celeriac, spring onions) plus nuts (pine nuts) and just a little red meat, so it takes in three different major plant-food groups. In character, it is a classic shepherd's pie given a makeover with a crispy celeriac rosti in place of the mash, ticking the Beyond potatoes (see page 147) box too, and is lower in carbs as a result. A bottle of tomato ketchup and Worcestershire sauce on the table are still *de rigeur*.

1. Heat 1 tablespoon of oil in a medium saucepan over a medium heat and fry the shallots and garlic for several minutes until softened. Add the mince and cook stirring until it changes colour and separates. Add the spices, chilli, wine, passata and some salt, bring to a simmer, cover and cook over a low heat for 15 minutes.

2. Meanwhile bring a large pan of salted water to the boil and cook the broad beans according to the packet instructions, then drain into a colander or sieve.

3. Skim off any excess fat from the sauce, and stir in the broad beans, pine nuts, olives and coriander. Transfer the mixture to a large shallow ovenproof dish (7 x 25 x 35cm/ 2.75 x 10 x 14in), which will allow plenty of crispy golden top. The pie base can be prepared up to 24 hours in advance, in which case leave to cool, then cover and chill until required.

4. Preheat the oven to 210°C (fan 190°C/gas mark 6), and coarsely grate the celeriac using the attachment on a food processor. Transfer the grated celeriac to a large bowl, drizzle over 2 tablespoons of oil, season and toss to coat it. Scatter this evenly over the pie base and gently press down to level it, then drizzle over 1 tablespoon of oil.

5. Toss the spring onions and cherry tomatoes with 1 tablespoon of oil and scatter over the surface. Cook the pie for 40–45 minutes until golden and crispy.

TIP

Keep an eye on the spring onions and cherry tomatoes while the pie is cooking. If they are colouring too quickly, cover the pie with foil.

SERVES 6

READY IN 2 HOURS 30 MINUTES

FLEXITARIAN

CASSOULET WITH WALNUT CRUMBS

- **approximately 5 tbsp extra virgin olive oil**
- **sea salt and freshly ground black pepper**
- **400g pork fillet, sliced into 1cm (½in) thick medallions**
- **1 medium white or yellow onion, peeled and chopped**
- **1 celery heart, sliced**
- **500g courgettes, trimmed, halved lengthways and sliced**
- **1 tsp smoked paprika**
- **100g sun-dried tomatoes, diced**
- **1 x 400g tin chopped tomatoes**
- **3 x 400g tins haricot or cannellini beans, drained and rinsed**
- **600ml chicken stock**
- **1 bay leaf**
- **2 garlic cloves, peeled and smashed**
- **50g fresh wholemeal breadcrumbs**
- **50g finely chopped walnuts**

A cassoulet is well known for both its hearty relaxed style, and the time it takes to prepare. Even once you reach the finishing line, the result can be a tad dry and heavy. Hence this soupy take on it, that comes dripping with juices – take a fork to mash the beans for pure comfort eating. Some crisp wholemeal breadcrumbs spliced with nuts are scattered over at the end.

1. Preheat the oven to 160°C (140°C fan/gas mark 3). Heat 1 teaspoon of oil in a large non-stick frying pan over a medium heat, season the pork slices on one side and fry on each side to colour them – you will probably need to do this in batches.

2. Heat 2 tablespoons of oil in a large flameproof casserole dish over a medium heat, add the onion, celery and courgette and fry for about 10 minutes until glossy and starting to colour, stirring frequently, and adding the paprika 1 minute before the end. Stir in the sun-dried tomatoes, the tinned tomatoes, the beans, the stock, the bay leaf, the garlic and some salt, then add the pork and any juices. Cover and pop into the oven for 2 hours.

3. Towards the end of this time, heat 2 tablespoons of oil in a large non-stick frying pan over a medium heat. Add the breadcrumbs and nuts and fry for about 5 minutes until golden and crisp, stirring almost constantly. Drain on a double thickness of kitchen towel. These can be served warm or at room temperature.

4. Serve the cassoulet with the crumbs scattered over.

SERVES 6–8

READY IN 50 MINUTES

VEGETARIAN

SPINACH, NUT AND GOAT'S CHEESE PIE

900g spinach
100g roasted cashews
100g toasted flaked almonds
finely grated zest of 1 lemon
2 tsp fresh thyme leaves
sea salt and freshly ground black pepper
3 tbsp extra virgin olive oil
4 tbsp fresh wholemeal breadcrumbs
200g goat's cheese, e.g. Chevre Log, rind discarded and sliced

This lovely creamy pie, cooked as a cake and served in slices, is inspired by the nut roasts of old, and makes for a great veggie main.

1. Bring a large pan of salted water to the boil, add the spinach, bring back to the boil and cook for 2 minutes, then drain into the colander and leave to cool.

2. Press out as much water as you can from the spinach using your hands, then slice or chop it. Place it in a large bowl, chop and add the cashews, almonds, lemon zest, thyme, some seasoning and 2 tablespoons of olive oil and stir to combine.

3. Toss the breadcrumbs with the remaining tablespoon of oil and scatter half over the base of a 20cm (8in) round loose-based cake tin, at least 4cm (1½in) deep. Press half the spinach mixture on top, then lay over the goat's cheese and repeat with the remaining spinach, then scatter with the rest of the breadcrumbs. You can prepare the pie to this point in advance, in which case cover and chill it. It may take a little longer to cook.

4. Preheat the oven to 210°C (fan 190°C/gas mark 6) and cook the pie for 30 minutes until golden and crisp on the surface. Serve in wedges.

ROOT VEG AND APPLE PIE

SERVES 6

READY IN 1 HOUR 30 MINUTES

VEGAN

- 600g carrots, trimmed, peeled and finely sliced
- 600g celeriac, skin cut off, cut downwards into wedges and finely sliced
- 4 tbsp extra virgin olive oil
- 2 garlic cloves, peeled and finely chopped
- 2 tsp finely chopped fresh rosemary needles, plus a few extra needles
- sea salt and freshly ground black pepper
- 2 red-skinned eating apples, quartered, cored and thinly sliced lengthways

A delectably sweet layered pie, which would be lovely with the Haricot bean smash (see page 154). Try to slice the vegetables as thinly as possible to avoid gaps when you layer them – this is best done by hand. Vegetarians or flexitarians could also scatter some grated cheese, such as Gruyère, Abondance or Comté, between the carrot and celeriac layers.

1. Preheat the oven to 200°C (fan 180°C/gas mark 6). Toss the carrot and celeriac separately in large bowls each with 1½ tablespoons of olive oil, half the garlic, half the chopped rosemary, and some seasoning.

2. Arrange the celeriac in a layer in a 20 x 30cm (8 x 12in) shallow ovenproof dish. Layer the carrot on top, cover tightly with foil and bake for 50 minutes or until the vegetables are tender when pierced with a knife.

3. Scatter the apple and the extra rosemary needles over the surface, drizzle over the remaining oil and return to the oven for 15 minutes, then pop under the grill, preheated to high, to colour the top.

SERVES 6

READY IN 1 HOUR 45 MINUTES

FLEXITARIAN

CHICKEN AND MUSHROOM PIE WITH CAULIFLOWER MASH

- approximately 4 tbsp extra virgin olive oil
- sea salt and freshly ground black pepper
- approximately 1.1kg skin-on, bone-in free-range chicken thighs
- 150ml white wine
- 250ml chicken stock or water
- 50g unsalted butter
- 700g large white or yellow onions, peeled, halved and sliced
- 1kg small cauliflower florets
- freshly grated nutmeg to season
- 200g button mushrooms, stalks trimmed and halved
- 4 tbsp coarsely chopped fresh flat-leaf parsley
- 30g fresh wholemeal breadcrumbs

Chicken and mushroom pie is on repeat request in my house, a home-coming reminder of nostalgic comfort food. Actually it's not just pie, chicken and mushroom pasta, chicken and mushroom pot-roast, any which way. So a pie with a healthy spin on the potato/pastry surround was the goal here, and the cauliflower mash is every bit as silky as the usual, while an onion sauce replaces a gloopy white one, with oodles of flavour.

1. Cook the chicken, onions and cauliflower at the same time. For the chicken heat 1 teaspoon of olive oil in a large flameproof casserole dish over a medium-high heat, season the chicken thighs and colour them on both sides, half at a time. Drain off the fat, return all the chicken thighs to the pan, add the wine and simmer to reduce by half. Pour in the chicken stock or water. Bring to a simmer, cover and cook over a low heat for 30 minutes, stirring halfway through.

2. For the onions, melt 30g butter in a large saucepan over a low heat. Add the onions, sprinkle over 1 teaspoon of sea salt and gently fry over a very low heat for 30 minutes, stirring frequently to prevent them colouring. By the end they should be lusciously silky and soft.

3. Place the cauliflower in another large saucepan with 150ml water, dot with the remaining butter, add 1 tablespoon of olive oil and some salt. Bring the liquid to a simmer, then cover and cook over a low heat for

continued overleaf ▶

25–30 minutes until very tender, stirring halfway through. Discarding any residual liquid, reduce the cauliflower to a purée in a food processor, seasoning it with nutmeg and more salt if necessary. You tend to get the best results if you do this in a couple of batches.

4. Meanwhile, heat 1 tablespoon of oil in a large non-stick frying pan over a medium-high heat and fry the mushrooms for several minutes until lightly coloured, stirring occasionally, then transfer to a medium bowl.

5. Remove the chicken pieces to a bowl and leave the juices to settle, the fat will rise to the top. Once the chicken is cool enough to handle, remove and discard the skin and coarsely shred the flesh. Skim any fat off the surface of the cooking juices, and purée 150ml of these in a blender with the onions. Combine the chicken with the sauce in a large bowl and mix in the mushrooms and parsley.

6. Transfer this to a shallow ovenproof dish, approximately 20 x 30cm (8 x 12in). The filling and mash can be prepared well in advance, in which case leave to cool, then cover and chill.

7. To cook the pie, preheat the oven to 210°C (fan 190°C/gas mark 6). Spread the cauliflower mash over the pie filling and fork into a criss-cross pattern. Toss the breadcrumbs with 1 tablespoon of oil and scatter over the mash. Bake the pie for 40 minutes until the crumbs are lightly coloured, then pop under a grill, preheated to high, for a few minutes to crisp the crumbs further.

SERVES 6

READY IN 2 HOURS 30 MINUTES

FLEXITARIAN

CHILLI BEEF PIE WITH AUBERGINE

FOR THE FILLING

sea salt and freshly ground black pepper
400g lean braising beef (e.g. chuck or blade), cut into 3–4cm (1¼–1½in) pieces
approximately 5 tbsp extra virgin olive oil
1 red onion, peeled and chopped
2 red peppers, core and seeds removed, cut into thin strips, 5–7cm (2–2¾in) long
3 garlic cloves, peeled and finely sliced
1 tsp smoked paprika
1 tsp ground cumin
1 tsp dried mint or oregano
1 x 400g tin chopped tomatoes
1 x 400g tin chickpeas, drained and rinsed
1 x 200g tin sweetcorn, drained and rinsed

A beef hotpot is on the top ten list of favourite meaty dishes from around the world. This rendition is deeply savoury with the comforting warmth of chilli, while the roast aubergines and onions on top melt into the stew below. If you have a particular penchant for either sweetcorn or chickpeas, then you can add a few more as preferred.

1. Heat a large flameproof casserole dish over a medium heat, season the beef, add 1 tablespoon of oil to the dish and colour half the beef on all sides, remove the pieces to a bowl and cook the remainder in the same way, adding another tablespoon of oil.

2. Tip out any residual fat, add another tablespoon of oil, turn the heat down a little and fry the onion and peppers for 6–8 minutes until starting to colour, stirring occasionally. Stir in the garlic, spices, and mint or oregano and fry a couple of minutes longer until fragrant. Add the tinned tomatoes, 150ml water and stir the beef into the sauce. Bring to a simmer, then cover and cook over a low heat for 1¼ hours, stirring a couple of times to ensure it isn't sticking.

3. Stir the chickpeas and sweetcorn into the stew. Transfer to a shallow ovenproof dish, approximately 20 x 30cm (8 x 12in). The filling can be made well in advance, in which case leave to cool, then cover and chill.

continued overleaf ▶

FOR THE TOPPING

2 aubergines (approximately 500g), trimmed and cut into 1cm (½in) slices
300g red onions, peeled, halved and thinly sliced

TO SERVE

finely sliced medium-hot red chilli
coarsely chopped coriander

4. Meanwhile, preheat the oven to 210°C (fan 190°C/gas mark 6). Lay the aubergine slices out on a baking sheet, brushing with oil on both sides, and seasoning the top. Roast for 20 minutes, then turn the slices and cook for another 20 minutes until golden.

5. Lay the aubergine slices on top of the stew, toss the onion slices with 1 tablespoon of oil in a large bowl, separating out the strands, and scatter over the top of the aubergine. Bake, uncovered, for 35–45 minutes until the onions on top are golden and crisp. Scatter over a little chilli and coriander to serve.

SERVES 6

READY IN 1 HOUR 20 MINUTES

PESCATARIAN

FISH PIE WITH PECAN CRUMBLE

FOR THE FILLING

- 1 tbsp extra virgin olive oil
- 1 small dried red chilli, finely chopped
- 4 garlic cloves, peeled and finely chopped
- 2 fennel bulbs, green shoots and tough outer sheath discarded, diced
- 2 x 400g tins chopped tomatoes
- 3 tbsp coarsely chopped fresh flat-leaf parsley, plus extra to serve
- sea salt and freshly ground black pepper
- 600g skinless salmon fillets, cut into 3–4cm (1¼–1½in) pieces
- 200g butter beans, drained and rinsed

FOR THE CRUMBLE

- 30g pecans
- 30g ground almonds
- 30g rolled oats
- 30g unsalted butter, chilled and diced

This fish pie is lovely and light: salmon in a rich tomato and fennel sauce, with butter beans, and a delicate mixed nut and oat crumble on top in lieu of pastry or potato.

1. Heat the olive oil in a medium saucepan over a medium heat, add the chilli and garlic. Moments later add the fennel and fry for several minutes until translucent and softened slightly. Add the tomatoes, parsley and some seasoning, bring to a simmer and cook for 25–30 minutes, stirring occasionally, until you have a thick sauce.

2. Heat a large non-stick frying pan over a high heat, season the salmon and briefly sear it, half at a time, to lightly colour on all sides. Gently fold the salmon and butter beans into the sauce, discarding any liquid given out by the fish, and transfer the mixture to a shallow ovenproof dish, approximately 20 x 30cm (8 x 12in). The filling can be prepared a couple of hours in advance, in which case cover and set aside in a cool place.

3. For the crumble, whizz the pecans until finely chopped in a food processor, then add the ground almonds, oats, the butter and a little seasoning and briefly whizz until the crumbs start to hold together in nibs. This can also be made in advance, and chilled.

4. Preheat the oven to 210°C (fan 190°C/gas mark 6), scatter the crumble over the pie base and bake for about 30 minutes until the crumble is lightly golden. Serve scattered with extra parsley.

SERVES 6

READY IN 2 HOURS 15 MINUTES

FLEXITARIAN

IRISH STEW PIE

FOR THE STEW

1 sprig of fresh rosemary
600g lamb neck fillet, cut into 1–2cm (½–¾in) slices
3 medium white or yellow onions, peeled, halved and thinly sliced
1 celery heart, trimmed and thinly sliced
80g pearl barley
sea salt and freshly ground black pepper
200ml white wine
1 litre chicken stock

FOR THE TOPPING

1kg carrots, trimmed, peeled and thinly sliced (see Tip)
2–3 tbsp groundnut oil
coarsely chopped fresh flat-leaf parsley to serve

Here the reassurance of an Irish stew is turned into a pie with carrots as a crust, while the lamb broth is studded with barley, an overlooked whole grain in our search for new but ancient varieties.

1. The rosemary ideally needs to be wrapped in a small square of muslin or cotton sheet, which will prevent you from biting on the needles; alternatively, empty out a teabag to serve as a pouch. Layer the lamb, onions, celery and barley in a large flameproof casserole dish, seasoning the ingredients as you go, and tucking in the rosemary. Pour over the wine and chicken stock, and level the ingredients to submerge them. Bring to the boil and skim off any foam on the surface, then cover and cook over a low heat for 1 hour.

2. Leave to sit for 10 minutes, then skim off the surface fat, pour as much of the residual liquid as possible through a sieve into a medium saucepan, bring to the boil and cook to reduce by about a third to concentrate the flavour. Discard the rosemary pouch and pour the liquid back over the lamb.

3. Preheat the oven to 210°C (fan 190°C/gas mark 6). Toss the carrot with 2 tablespoons of oil and some seasoning, in a large bowl, and arrange in a layer on top of the pie, then drizzle over a little more oil. Bake in the oven for about 40 minutes until starting to colour, then pop under a grill, preheated to high, for a few minutes until the carrots char at the edges. Serve the pie with plenty of parsley scattered over.

TIP

The quickest route to thinly slice this quantity of carrots is to use the attachment on a food processor, and to finish slicing any ends by hand.

SERVES 4

READY IN 1 HOUR 30 MINUTES

FLEXITARIAN

ROAST CHICKEN AND ROOTS WITH PERSILLADE

FOR THE ROAST CHICKEN AND VEGETABLES

500g celeriac, skin cut off and sliced into 1–2cm (½–¾in) thick chips
400g beetroot, trimmed and cut into wedges
400g carrots, trimmed and cut into two shorter lengths and into 1–2cm (½–¾in) thick chips
4 tbsp extra virgin olive oil
sea salt and freshly ground black pepper
4 skin-on, bone-in free-range chicken thighs (approximately 600g)
½ tsp finely grated lemon zest, plus juice of 1 lemon
75g black or green lentils

FOR THE PERSILLADE

20g fresh flat-leaf parsley leaves, finely chopped
2 garlic cloves, peeled and finely chopped

No need to peel the veggies here. You can also roast drumsticks in lieu of the thighs; allow a couple per person. The veggies make for a gorgeous blast of colour and of flavour – one-pan cooking at its best.

1. Preheat the oven to 210°C (fan 190°C/gas mark 6). Arrange the vegetables in a large roasting tin that will hold them in a crowded single layer. Drizzle 3 tablespoons of oil over the vegetables, season and toss to coat. Roast for 30 minutes, then turn them, toss the chicken pieces with the remaining oil, season and tuck skin-side up between the veggies.

2. Drizzle over the lemon juice and roast for another 40–45 minutes until golden.

3. Meanwhile, bring a medium pan of water to the boil and cook the lentils for about 25 minutes or until just tender, then drain. For the persillade, combine the parsley, garlic and lemon zest in a small bowl.

4. Place the chicken on four plates. Stir the lentils into the veggies and spoon this beside the chicken, and scatter with the persillade.

VEGAN SWAP

Replace the chicken thighs with the Fiery chickpea dip (page 134) and a green salad with avocado.

SERVES 4

READY IN 1 HOUR 10 MINUTES

FLEXITARIAN

CRISPY CHICKEN THIGHS WITH FIERY CHICKPEA DIP

FOR THE CHICKEN

3 small sprigs of fresh rosemary
2 garlic cloves, peeled and crushed to a paste
1 tbsp extra virgin olive oil
4 skin-on, bone-in free-range chicken thighs
sea salt and freshly ground black pepper
15g unsalted butter, softened

FOR THE DIP

75g hazelnuts
1 x 400g tin chickpeas, drained and rinsed
½ garlic clove, peeled
⅓ tsp cayenne pepper, plus a little extra for dusting
3 tbsp lemon juice
1 tbsp extra virgin olive oil
micro leaves or salad sprouts to serve

This feisty dip is a variation on the theme of a hummus, and the nuts and chickpeas balance out the smaller quantity of chicken. Build it into your favourite roast, with, for instance, the Celeriac wedges (page 162) or Honey and sesame roast roots (page 159).

1. Preheat the oven to 210°C (fan 190°C/gas mark 6). Pull half the needles off the rosemary sprigs and combine these and the rosemary stalks in a large bowl with the garlic and oil.

2. Add the chicken thighs and turn to coat them, then season with salt and pepper. Place the thighs, skin-side up, in a roasting tin with a little space between each thigh, and evenly distributing the rosemary, smear a little butter over the top of each one. Roast for 50 minutes until golden and crisp, then leave to rest for 10 minutes.

3. Meanwhile make the dip. Whizz the nuts in a food processor to finely chop them, then continue to whizz to a nut butter, scraping down the bowl as necessary. Add the chickpeas, garlic, cayenne pepper and some salt and whizz to a coarse paste, then gradually add 75ml water, the lemon juice and olive oil through the funnel. The dip should be the consistency of mayonnaise so, if necessary, add a little more water. Spoon the mixture into a bowl.

4. Serve the chicken thighs with the dip to the side, dusted with a little cayenne and piled with micro leaves or salad sprouts.

SERVES 4

READY IN 35–40 MINUTES

VEGAN

ROAST ROMANESCO AND SPRING ONION SALAD WITH BALSAMIC DRESSING

- 1 x Romanesco, cut into florets (approximately 400g)
- 4 jumbo or 8 standard spring onions, trimmed and cut diagonally into 2–3cm (¾–1¼in) lengths
- 4 tbsp hempseed or nut oil
- sea salt and freshly ground black pepper
- 150g cherry tomatoes, quartered
- 2 tsp balsamic vinegar
- 1 tbsp small capers (*nonpareille*), rinsed
- 2 handfuls of lamb's lettuce
- 2 tbsp chopped Brazil nuts
- 1 tsp fresh lemon thyme leaves

The recommendation to rely on vegetable oils rather than saturated fats, comes with endless variety, and the choice on offer gets better and better. I am warming up to hempseed, which bridges the divide between the full-on aroma of hazelnut and the more discreet scent of rapeseed. Any nutty oil will serve you well here.

You can also make this salad with classic broccoli florets, but Romanesco with its spiralling minarets is always a show-stopper. This can stand in as a 'roast' for vegans and vegetarians, I would add in a second dish of a pulse or whole grains for satiety.

1. Preheat the oven to 210°C (fan 190°C/gas mark 6). Arrange the Romanesco florets and spring onions in a large roasting tin that holds them snugly in a single layer. Drizzle over half the oil, season and toss to coat, then roast for 20–25 minutes until lightly golden, stirring halfway through. Leave to cool.

2. Toss the tomatoes with a little salt and set aside for 15 minutes. Stir in the balsamic vinegar, the remaining oil and the capers. Transfer the roast veg to a large serving dish and mix in the lamb's lettuce. Spoon over the tomato mixture and scatter over the Brazil nuts and thyme.

SERVES 4

READY IN 45–55 MINUTES

VEGETARIAN

SPICY CAULI WITH TURMERIC YOGHURT

700g small cauliflower florets, approximately 2–3cm/¾–1¼in
1 red onion, peeled, halved and thinly sliced across
3 tbsp extra virgin olive oil
2 tbsp lemon juice
sea salt
1 heaped tsp coriander seeds, coarsely ground
1 heaped tsp cumin seeds, coarsely ground
40g buckwheat
1 large handful of coarsely chopped fresh mint
1 large handful of coarsely chopped fresh flat-leaf parsley

FOR THE TURMERIC YOGHURT

150g zero-fat Greek yoghurt
1 tbsp soured cream
½ tsp finely grated lemon zest, plus 1 tsp lemon juice
pinch of ground turmeric
½ tsp ground sumac
pomegranate seeds to serve

Like so many roast veggie dishes this is endlessly versatile; eat it any temperature you like, and it will still be delicious cold the next day. Buckwheat is one of the healthiest grains, with a complete set of all nine essential amino acids. This also goes well with a lamb cutlet or two (page 140), if you are planning your weekly meat treat. Vegans can replace the yoghurt with a dollop of coconut yoghurt.

1. Preheat the oven to 210°C (fan 190°C/gas mark 6). Spread the cauliflower over the base of a large roasting tin, then mix in the onion separating out the slices. Drizzle over the olive oil and lemon juice and stir to coat, then season with salt, scatter over the coriander and cumin seeds and stir again. Roast for 30–40 minutes until golden at the edges and crests, stirring halfway through. Leave to cool to an ambient temperature.

2. In the meantime, bring a medium pan of water to the boil, add the buckwheat and simmer for 15–20 minutes or until tender, then drain into a colander.

3. While the veg and buckwheat are cooking, blend all the turmeric yoghurt ingredients together in a small bowl with a little salt and set aside.

4. Mix the herbs into the cauliflower, also the buckwheat and a little more salt. Transfer this to a large serving dish. Serve with the turmeric yoghurt dolloped on top, scattered with pomegranate seeds.

SERVES 2

READY IN 40 MINUTES

FLEXITARIAN

CHICKEN WITH SPINACH AND PADRÓN PEPPERS

- **3 tbsp rapeseed oil**
- **2 tsp dark soy sauce**
- **juice ½ lemon**
- **3 garlic cloves, peeled and crushed to a paste**
- **2 skinless free-range chicken breast fillets (approximately 90–100g per fillet; see Tip)**
- **100g padrón peppers**
- **sea salt**
- **5g unsalted butter**
- **150g spinach**

The chicken cooks in a deliciously savoury marinade, for sheer punch a little chicken goes a long way. For a more substantial dish, you could also stir 100g of cooked black or green lentils into the wilted spinach.

1. Combine 2 tablespoons of oil, the soy sauce, lemon juice and garlic in a large bowl. Add the chicken fillets and stir to coat them. Place the chicken fillets and marinade in a medium saucepan (e.g. 20cm), cover and cook for 7 minutes over a low heat, then turn the fillets and cook for another 7 minutes.

2. Transfer them to a plate and simmer the marinade until the garlic starts to darken, then return the breasts to the pan and cook for another few minutes, turning them over, until they are lightly coloured and the garlic is deliciously caramelized.

3. Transfer the fillets back to the plate and spoon the caramelized garlic on top, leaving behind the oil. Leave to rest for 5–10 minutes while you cook the vegetables.

4. Heat a large non-stick frying over a medium-high heat, add a trickle of oil and fry the padrón peppers for about 5 minutes until lightly golden, seasoning them with a pinch of salt and tossing frequently. Transfer these to a bowl, add the butter to the pan and fry the spinach until it wilts.

5. Divide the spinach between 2 plates, place the chicken on top (slicing it if wished), and pile with the padrón peppers.

continued overleaf ▶

TIP

If your chicken breasts come up larger than the specified weight, trim them and freeze the trimmings. These can be fried up in a stir-fry or used at a later date.

GET AHEAD

The chicken can be marinated on the morning of the day you are having dinner, in which case cover and chill.

VEGAN SWAP

Replace the chicken with this Teriyaki tofu.

200g firm tofu
1 heaped tsp cornflour, sifted
⅓ tsp 5-spice powder
sea salt
1 tbsp toasted sesame oil
1 tbsp teriyaki
squeeze of lemon or lime juice
sesame seeds for sprinkling

1. Press the tofu block between double layers of kitchen towel to absorb the excess liquid, changing the paper once or twice as necessary, then cut the block into 1cm (½in) dice.

2. Combine the cornflour, spice blend and some salt in a large bowl, add the tofu and toss to coat.

3. Heat a large non-stick frying pan over a high heat for a couple of minutes, add the oil and then the tofu and fry for 6–8 minutes, stirring frequently until golden. Drizzle over the teriyaki and cook for another minute until the tofu is dark and crisp at the edges.

4. Serve with a squeeze of lemon or lime juice, scattered with sesame seeds.

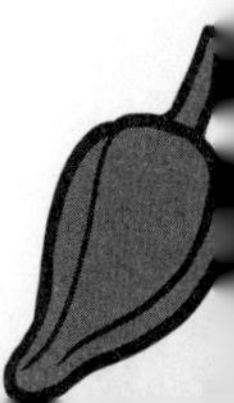

SERVES 2

READY IN 40–50 MINUTES

FLEXITARIAN

RACK OF LAMB WITH PESTO POTATOES

approximately 1 tbsp extra virgin olive oil
1 x 4 chop rack of lamb
sea salt and freshly ground black pepper
175g baby new potatoes
175g fresh peas (see Tip)
2 tbsp pesto

As roast lamb has always been my husband's favourite supper, once our children dissipated it presented something of a problem. There is little point in roasting up an enormous joint for two of you. At this point we settled on a rack of lamb as being the answer, which also happens to fulfil the call for less meat, being so sweet and delicate it makes for a small luxury.

A couple of delicate lamb cutlets come well within the recommendation, and racks can be sized to fit any number of people, simply ask for the number of chops you want. As someone with a light appetite, I am happy with just one chop, savouring every mouthful. There are some excellent fresh pestos in the chill cabinet, check the ingredient list, the fewer the better.

1. Preheat the oven to 230°C (210°C fan/gas mark 8). Drizzle a little oil over the rack and season the fat. Heat a non-stick frying pan over a medium-high heat and colour the fat. Place the rack, fat-side down, in a small roasting tin and roast for about 25 minutes for rare or 30 minutes for medium, then transfer to a warm plate to rest for 10–15 minutes.

2. At the same time as cooking the lamb, bring a large pan of salted water to the boil, add the potatoes and simmer for about 20 minutes or until just tender, then add the peas and cook for another 3 minutes. Drain them into a colander and leave for a few minutes for the surface moisture to evaporate.

3. Return the potatoes and peas to the pan, then partly crush and partly chop them using a potato masher. Spoon over the pesto, drizzle over 2 teaspoons of oil, season and gently toss.

4. Carve the lamb into chops and serve on top of the crushed potatoes, drizzled with any juices from the resting lamb.

TIP

You can also use frozen peas, in which case bring the water back to the boil before cooking for 3 minutes.

SERVES 4

READY IN 45 MINUTES

VEGAN (WITHOUT THE MUSTARD CREAM)

ROAST BEETROOT AND ASPARAGUS ROAST

200g black rice
400g small beetroot
5 tbsp extra virgin olive oil
1 tsp fresh lemon thyme leaves
½ tsp fennel seeds, coarsely ground
sea salt and freshly ground black pepper
300g thick asparagus (trimmed weight, approximately 500g whole), halved into shorter lengths
3 garlic cloves, peeled and crushed to a paste
2 tsp lemon juice
2 tsp balsamic vinegar
1 handful of coarsely chopped fresh flat-leaf parsley
Mustard cream to serve (optional, see Tip)

Here a tray of beetroot is roasted with fennel seeds and garlic and married with roast asparagus at the end. The veg are combined with black rice, which is delicious stuff, once reserved for royalty in ancient China, such was its value. But any nutty unrefined variety will do, including wild rice. This is delicious served with smoked fish such as salmon or eel, and also pickled anchovies.

1. Bring a medium pan of water to the boil and cook the rice for 35 minutes until tender, or according to the packet instructions, then drain into a sieve.

2. Meanwhile, preheat the oven to 240°C (fan 220°C/gas mark 9). Trim the shoots off the beetroots, and cut off the whiskery tail, then slice into slim wedges. Place in a large bowl and toss with half the olive oil, thyme, fennel and some seasoning. Spread over the base of a large roasting tin.

3. Spread the asparagus over the base of another large roasting tin, drizzle over the remaining oil, season and toss to coat.

4. Roast the vegetables for 15 minutes, with the asparagus on the upper shelf and the beetroot below.

5. Scatter the garlic over the beetroot and give both trays of vegetables a stir. Roast the asparagus for a further 5 minutes, then drizzle over the lemon juice. Roast the beetroot for another 15 minutes, and drizzle over the balsamic vinegar.

6. Combine the two trays and fold in the rice. The vegetables are delicious hot or cold, mix in the parsley shortly before serving. Accompany with the Mustard cream, if wished.

TIP

A dollop of Mustard cream adds an extra flavour dimension to the roast veg – place 50g crème fraîche or soured cream in a small dish and stir 1 tsp Dijon mustard through, to streak it. Cover and chill until required.

SERVES 4

READY IN 1 HOUR 25 MINUTES

VEGETARIAN

ROAST CELERIAC, CARROT AND APPLE

A pesto made with spinach and walnuts elevates a humble selection of root veg, and apple provides a lively sourness. You want carrots that are no bigger than your little finger. Vegans can omit the pesto or leave out the cheese and whizz up a simple herb purée.

FOR THE ROAST VEGETABLES AND APPLE

400g celeriac, skin cut off and sliced into chunky chips, 1–2cm (½–¾ in) thick
400g small Chantenay carrots, stalk-ends trimmed
400g eating apples, quartered, cored and cut into thin segments
4 bulbs of garlic, tops cut off to reveal the cloves
3–4 rosemary sprigs, 5–7cm (2–2¾in) long
3 medium-hot red chillies
4 tbsp extra virgin olive oil
sea salt and freshly ground black pepper

FOR THE PESTO

20g walnuts
50g baby spinach leaves
3 tbsp extra virgin olive oil
15g grated vegetarian Parmesan-style cheese

1. Preheat the oven to 210°C (fan 190°C/gas mark 6). Arrange the vegetables, apple, garlic, rosemary and chillies in a large roasting tin that will hold them in a crowded single layer. Drizzle the olive oil over the vegetables, season with salt and pepper and toss to coat. Roast for 70–75 minutes until golden, turning with a spatula halfway through.

2. While they are cooking make the pesto. Whizz the walnuts in a food processor to finely chop, then add the spinach and olive oil and whizz to a purée. Add the cheese and a little salt and briefly whizz again. Serve the vegetables hot or warm, dolloped with the pesto.

SERVES 4

READY IN 1 HOUR 15 MINUTES

VEGAN

MISO-GLAZED COURGETTE AND PEPPERS

30g red miso
10g golden caster sugar
1 scant tbsp sake
1 scant tbsp mirin
3 tbsp rapeseed oil
600g courgettes, trimmed and thickly sliced
4 long red peppers, core and seeds removed, cut into strips 6–7cm (2½–2¾in) long
150g frozen soya (edamame) beans
1 spring onion, trimmed, halved lengthways and thinly sliced
2 tsp toasted sesame seeds or flax seeds

Miso-glazed black cod is a dish that resides in some hallowed celestial chamber; I have been trying to make it for years, but it is never as good as the original. Which doesn't stop me trying and extending the glaze to all manner of other ingredients. So this isn't quite up there with those exquisitely buttery flakes of cod, but it's a very tasty plate of goodness. And as well as being an excellent vegan dish, this goes a treat with pan-fried seabass or seabream fillets.

1. Combine the miso, sugar, sake, mirin and 1 tablespoon of oil in a small saucepan and gently heat through, whisking or stirring to blend the ingredients. This can be made several hours in advance, in which case leave covered in the saucepan.

2. Preheat the oven to 210°C (fan 190°C/gas mark 6). Combine the courgettes and peppers in a large roasting tin, drizzle over the remaining oil, and toss to lightly coat them using your hands. Roast for 30 minutes until lightly golden, then drizzle over the miso marinade and roast for a further 30 minutes until a deep gold, stirring halfway through.

3. Meanwhile, bring a medium pan of water to the boil and cook the beans according to the packet instructions, then drain them into a sieve.

4. Mix the beans into the roast vegetables and transfer to a large serving plate. Scatter over the spring onion and sesame or flax seeds. Serve straightaway.

BEYOND POTATOES

FIFTY GRAMS OF POTATO A DAY, AS RECOMMENDED BY THE Planetary Health Diet, is meagre even by Dickensian workhouse standards. One small potato. On a daily basis that amounts to about five chips, a lonely roast potato or heaped teaspoon of mash. For those of us who have treated potatoes like a staple, eating them almost daily and without constraint, the new recommendations present a serious challenge. So this chapter is about finding ways around this, without having to relinquish our favourite ways of eating spuds. A part of this is to introduce more wholegrain sides, but also to make use of a much richer selection of vegetables for mash, roast and chips.

One question that will niggle many, raised to look upon a baked potato in its skin as an excellent source of fibre, vitamins and minerals, is 'why?'. Are we supposed to be cutting down on potatoes on environmental grounds or on nutrition grounds? The reasoning behind the reduction is more to do with health than damage to the ecosystem. The rationale, as explained by Professor Walter Willett, co-chair of the EAT–*Lancet* Commission, is that potatoes are associated with a higher risk of cardiometabolic disease when compared to whole grains. So yes, a little is fine, but they are not an optimal staple, especially for people who are not lean and active, which can cause low insulin sensitivity, also known as insulin resistance. This is when cells fail to absorb as much glucose, which can lead to high blood-sugar levels; this can, in turn, lead to type 2 diabetes.

Professor Willett explains further in his seminal book *Eat, Drink and Be Healthy* (that I would highly recommend reading as an adjunct to this), that whole grains are considerably richer in fibre and more nutrient dense than white potatoes. Also, we rapidly turn the starch in white potatoes to sugar, which causes a spike in blood sugar and insulin, whereas we digest whole grains more slowly, and this makes for a more even and lower rise in blood sugar.

There is also the issue of how we consume starchy veg, and not only in the West. In Africa, a tuber like cassava, which is a traditional staple, is often refined into white flour rather than being consumed in its unrefined or whole state when it has a relatively low glycaemic index (GI). In poor regions, this sugar swell that is devoid of nutrients is further exacerbated by eating too little animal protein.

While back in Western kitchens, the issue is more to do with how our consumption has changed during the last half-century, going from the meat-and-two-veg model where they were served as a side that was part of a home-cooked meal, to being turned into ultra-processed ready snacks such as crisps, chips and waffles. If you are someone who is used to eating baked potatoes or including them in your diet regularly in a way that is healthy, then there is no reason for this to be discouraged. The recommendation to reduce consumption has more to do with mopping up bad habits such as visits to the chippie that amount to 'dinner', and a little too often, which leads to obesity. There again, we can all benefit from eating a wide variety of whole grains.

While this chapter is about looking beyond potatoes to what we can serve as sides to our favourite stews, curries and the like, these recipes can also be used by vegetarians and vegans to partner another vegetarian dish, taking you halfway to supper.

SERVES 4

READY IN 35–40 MINUTES

VEGAN

BULGUR WHEAT PILAF

2 tbsp olive oil
1 small white or yellow onion, peeled and chopped
225g bulgur wheat, rinsed in a sieve
150ml vegan white wine
300ml vegetable stock
sea salt and freshly ground black pepper
1 bay leaf
2 sprigs of fresh thyme

The texture of this pilaf succeeds in being bold and nutty, as well as light and ethereal. Dish it up with no further ado as the side to a stew, tagine or curry. It also makes for a stand-alone with a salad, or you could stir some savoury sautéed mushrooms into it.

1. Heat the olive oil in a medium-large saucepan over a medium heat and fry the onion for 5–10 minutes, stirring occasionally until it is soft and lightly coloured.

2. Add the bulgur wheat and stir to coat it with oil, then add the wine and stock and season generously with salt and pepper. Bring the liquid to the boil, add the herbs, cover with a tight-fitting lid and cook over a low heat for 10 minutes by which time all the liquid should have been absorbed.

3. Without removing the lid, remove from the heat and leave it for 15 minutes, during which time it will dry out further and become more tender. Fluff up with a fork and remove the herbs before serving.

VARIATION

COCKTAIL NUT PILAF

4 tbsp coarsely chopped fresh flat-leaf parsley
squeeze of lemon juice
100g roasted and salted mixed cocktail nuts – macadamias, almonds, cashews, Brazils, pecans, etc., coarsely chopped
chutney or salsa to serve

This is especially good around Christmas when luxurious cocktail nut mixes abound. At other times of the year, any roasted nut you have to hand can be put to good use.

1. Cook the pilaf as above, omitting the bay and thyme. Give the pilaf a stir to fluff up the bulgur wheat, toss in the parsley and season with a squeeze of lemon and more salt if necessary.

2. Serve the pilaf scattered with the chopped nuts. Accompany with whatever chutney or salsa takes your fancy.

SERVES 4

READY IN 45–50 MINUTES

VEGAN

LEMON AND PINE NUT BROWN RICE PILAF

250g brown basmati rice
2 tbsp vegetable oil, e.g. groundnut
4 shallots, peeled, halved and thinly sliced
50g pine nuts or raw cashews
1 cinnamon stick
8 green cardamom pods, smashed
4 cloves
2 bay leaves
2 strips of lemon zest (removed with a potato peeler)

Having grown up with white rice, I used to regard brown rice as inferior, whereas now I relish its flavour and alluringly toothsome bite. Here it is given a little added appeal with silky shallots and toasted nuts, spiced up with a handful of aromatics. Like the Bulgur wheat pilaf on page 150, this is a great base for anything that lies on the soupy side.

A brown rice pilaf benefits from a different method to white rice, by cooking it separately to the aromatics, and then combining them at the end and leaving the pilaf to steam and fluff up, taking up the scent of the spices and herbs. The addition of nuts, as with the Cocktail nut pilaf on page 151, provides a nutritional extra, adding a tad more protein into the mix which is another good way of redressing a slightly smaller amount of meat, fish or poultry in any dish.

1. Bring a medium-large pan of salted water to the boil, add the rice and cook for 25–30 minutes, until tender, or according to the packet instructions.

2. Five minutes before the end of the rice cooking time, heat the oil in a medium saucepan over a medium-low heat, add the shallots, nuts, spices, bay leaves and lemon zest and fry for about 5 minutes until lightly coloured, stirring almost constantly to make sure the nuts don't burn.

3. Drain the rice into a sieve and stir into this base, then cover and set aside for 20 minutes. It's quite good-natured and if you leave it a little longer than this it won't come to any harm.

TIPS FOR THE TABLE

From here you can serve it as is, or scattered with coriander and mint leaves, or crispy onions.

SERVES 6

READY IN 15 MINUTES

VEGAN

HARICOT BEAN SMASH

- approximately 6 tbsp extra virgin olive oil
- 3–4 banana shallots, peeled, halved and thinly sliced
- 3 x 400g tins cannellini or haricot beans, drained and rinsed
- squeeze of lemon juice
- sea salt and freshly ground black pepper

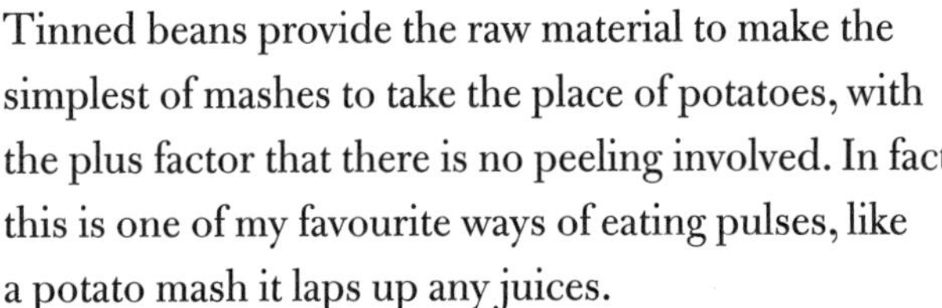

Tinned beans provide the raw material to make the simplest of mashes to take the place of potatoes, with the plus factor that there is no peeling involved. In fact this is one of my favourite ways of eating pulses, like a potato mash it laps up any juices.

Any creamy bean is good here, haricot and cannellini beans will make for a delicate ivory mash, while flageolet the palest green one. And the texture can be varied, coarsely mash the beans with a potato masher for a 'smashed' effect, or give them a whizz in a food processor like the Cannellini bean mash (opposite) if you want something smoother. Although this serves 6, it is readily scaled up or down.

1. Bring a medium pan of water to the boil. Heat 2 tablespoons of oil in a small saucepan over a medium heat, add the shallots and fry for 5–7 minutes, stirring occasionally, until golden.

2. Add the beans to the boiling water and blanch for a couple of minutes, then drain them into a sieve and return them to the pan. Coarsely mash with 3 tablespoons of oil, a squeeze of lemon juice and some seasoning, then stir in three quarters of the shallots.

3. Transfer the mash to a serving bowl, scatter the remaining shallots over and drizzle with a little more oil.

SERVES 6

READY IN 15 MINUTES

VEGAN

CANNELLINI BEAN MASH WITH ROAST PEPPERS

- 3 x 400g tins cannellini beans, drained and rinsed
- 5 tbsp extra virgin olive oil
- sea salt
- 1 tbsp lemon juice
- 2 banana shallots, peeled and finely chopped
- 1 garlic clove, peeled and finely chopped
- 1 x 400g jar roast peppers – I like Fragata – drained and sliced into thin strips 5–6cm (2–2½in) long
- ½ tsp ground cumin
- cayenne pepper to season
- 1 handful of coarsely chopped fresh flat-leaf parsley

This will make for the perfect side to the Aubergine-wrapped Greek sausages (see page 174) if you are after a Healthy Planet sausages and mash, but is also great with anything Moroccan such as the Lamb, date and tomato tagine (see page 88).

1. Combine the beans with 3 tablespoons of oil, 75ml water and some salt in a medium pan, bring to the boil, cover and gently heat through for a few minutes. Purée the contents of the pan in a food processor with the lemon juice.

2. Meanwhile, heat 2 tablespoons of olive oil in a medium saucepan over a medium heat and fry the shallots for about 5 minutes until lightly golden, stirring frequently and adding the garlic a minute before the end. Add the peppers, cumin, some salt and a little cayenne pepper and fry for a couple of minutes longer, then stir in the parsley.

3. Smooth the bean purée over the base of a shallow serving bowl and spoon the red pepper mixture on top.

SERVES 4

READY IN 15 MINUTES

VEGETARIAN

BEETROOT MASH WITH WILD MUSHROOMS

30g unsalted butter
4 banana shallots, peeled and finely chopped
400g cooked and peeled beetroot (unvinegared), diced
1 tsp balsamic vinegar
freshly grated nutmeg to season
sea salt and freshly ground black pepper
squeeze of lemon juice
1 tbsp extra virgin olive oil
200g wild and cultivated mushrooms, trimmed, torn or sliced as necessary

I do love the drama of a beetroot mash that looks as though it should be adorning some Renaissance table. Intended as an alternative to potato mash, it is lighter than pulse mashes and grain sides. This has a particular affinity with mackerel (see page 108). You can replace the butter with olive oil if wished, for a vegan mash, but it does add a lovely flavour.

1. For the beetroot purée, melt half the butter in a large non-stick frying pan over a medium-low heat, and fry half the shallots for a couple of minutes until softened and lightly coloured, stirring frequently. Add the beetroot and fry for another few minutes until glossy and buttery.

2. Purée the contents of the pan in a blender, with 50ml water, the balsamic vinegar, nutmeg and some seasoning, then sharpen with a squeeze of lemon juice. The purée can be made well in advance and gently reheated in the pan on the hob, stirring frequently.

3. At the same time heat another large non-stick frying pan over a medium-high heat, add the remaining butter and the olive oil, and briefly fry the remaining shallot until translucent. Throw in the mushrooms and fry for a few minutes, stirring occasionally until golden. If any liquid is given out, continue to fry until they are dry and coloured, and season at the end. Serve the beetroot purée, scattered with the mushrooms.

SERVES 6

READY IN 30 MINUTES

VEGAN

PEA AND MINT MASH

sea salt and freshly ground black pepper
500g baby new potatoes
500g fresh peas (see Tip)
4 tbsp extra virgin olive oil
1 tbsp lemon juice
3 tbsp finely chopped fresh mint

This mash is a positive take on eating less potatoes. By combining them half and half with peas, it is lower in carbs than white potatoes, while also rich in plant protein, again offsetting a smaller quantity of meat. As ever, peas, potatoes and mint are a fab mix with lamb, the perfect side to Rack of lamb (see page 140) instead of the pesto potatoes.

1. Bring a large pan of salted water to the boil, add the potatoes and simmer for about 20 minutes or until just tender, then add the peas and cook for another 3 minutes. Drain them into a colander and leave for a few minutes for the surface moisture to evaporate.

2. Return the potatoes and peas to the pan, then partly crush and partly chop them using a potato masher. Pour over the olive oil and lemon juice, scatter over the mint and plenty of seasoning and gently toss. The potatoes can be served straightaway or warm.

TIP

You can also use frozen peas, in which case bring the water back to the boil before cooking for 3 minutes.

SERVES 6

READY IN 25 MINUTES

VEGAN

BROCCOLI MASH WITH SESAME SEEDS

sea salt and freshly ground black pepper
900g broccoli florets
3 tbsp extra virgin olive oil, plus extra to serve
2 tbsp lemon juice, plus extra to serve
1 handful of fresh coriander, plus extra chopped to serve
20g toasted sesame seeds (see Tip)

Broccoli and cauliflower both make for excellent mashes that are low in carbohydrates. This one is enlivened with lemon, coriander and sesame seeds, and sits gracefully within most culture line-ups.

1. Bring a large pan of salted water to the boil and simmer the broccoli florets for about 15 minutes until really soft. Drain the broccoli into a colander, shaking it thoroughly, and leave for a few minutes to steam-dry.

2. Whizz the broccoli to a purée in a food processor with the olive oil, lemon juice, coriander and some seasoning. You may need to do this in batches.

3. Gently rewarm in a small pan on the hob, stirring frequently, then transfer the mash to a shallow serving bowl, swirling the surface. Drizzle with a little more oil and lemon juice, and scatter with the sesame seeds and some more coriander.

TIP

To toast sesame seeds, scatter them over the base of a medium frying pan over a medium heat and toast for a few minutes until a pale gold, stirring frequently.

SERVES 4

READY IN 1 HOUR–1 HOUR 10 MINUTES

VEGETARIAN

HONEY AND SESAME ROAST ROOTS

- 450–500g medium carrots, trimmed and halved lengthways
- 450–500g medium beetroot, shoots and roots trimmed to 1cm (½in), halved or quartered downwards
- 1 handful of bay leaves
- 3 tbsp extra virgin olive oil
- 2 tbsp cider vinegar
- sea salt and freshly ground black pepper
- 1 tbsp runny honey
- 15g sesame seeds

This is my go-to in lieu of roast potatoes, a rustic duo of root veggies, with minimal preparation. Both beetroot and carrots are a source of fibre, vitamins, minerals and antioxidants.

1. Preheat the oven to 220°C (fan 200°C/gas mark 7). Arrange the vegetables with the bay leaves in a roasting tin that holds them snugly in a single layer. Drizzle over the oil and vinegar, season and roast for 50–60 minutes. Halfway through give them a stir and baste, drizzle over the honey and scatter over the sesame seeds.

SERVES 4

READY IN 45–50 MINUTES

VEGAN

ROAST CABBAGE WITH ALMONDS

- ½ Savoy cabbage, base trimmed, outer leaves discarded
- 300g Brussels sprouts, bases trimmed, outer leaves discarded and halved downwards
- 1 red onion, peeled, halved and thinly sliced
- 4 tbsp extra virgin olive oil
- sea salt and freshly ground black pepper
- 2 tsp balsamic vinegar
- 50g roasted Marcona almonds

Roasting cabbage might sound unlikely but it's a great way of making what can be quite a sombre vegetable more exciting. And by combining with Brussels sprouts it also seems more lavish.

This makes a lovely light dish that is intended to replace roast potatoes. It can also be made more filling by adding some warm Puy lentils to the finished dish before scattering with almonds. Marcona almonds are especially yummy, but toasted flaked almonds, or indeed other roasted nuts, can be used in lieu.

1. Preheat the oven to 210°C (fan 190°C/gas mark 6). Cut the cabbage half into thin wedges, leaving them attached by the thick central stalk at the base; don't worry if some of the leaves separate out.

2. Arrange the Brussels and cabbage with the red onion in a large roasting tin, drizzle over the olive oil, season and toss to coat everything. Roast for 35–40 minutes, stirring halfway through, until golden and crispy at the edges.

3. Drizzle over the vinegar and gently turn to mix in. Serve scattered with toasted almonds.

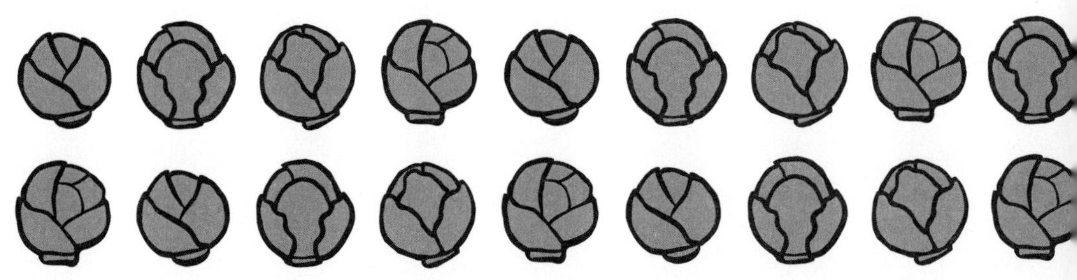

SERVES 4

READY IN 35–40 MINUTES

VEGETARIAN

COURGETTE CHIPS

1 medium free-range egg
approximately 1 tbsp extra virgin olive oil
sea salt
paprika to season
800g courgettes, ends trimmed, and cut into chips 1cm (½in) diameter and 5–7cm (2–2¾in) long
olive oil (for roasting) or vegetable oil (for frying)

These courgette chips are coated in a film of tempura-style batter to help them crisp. Bake them for a tender and creamy chip or fry them and they will be lacy at the edges. These are also low carb.

1. In a large bowl, whisk the egg with 1 tablespoon of olive oil, 1 tablespoon still or fizzy water, some salt and paprika.

2. Toss the courgette chips in the egg mixture to very lightly coat them. Use a slotted utensil to remove them from the bowl so that excess egg mixture is left behind.

To oven roast

Before dipping the courgettes, preheat the oven to 250°C (230°C fan/gas mark 9) and use a pastry brush to lightly coat the base of a couple of roasting tins with a thin film of olive oil. Scatter the dipped chips over the base of the tins in a single layer, and roast for 25–30 minutes until golden, turning them with a spatula halfway through. A lower tray will probably take longer than one on top.

To shallow fry

Heat about 1cm (½in) of vegetable oil in a large frying pan over a medium heat until a drop of the egg mixture sizzles when added. Fry the dipped chips, in batches, for a few minutes, turning them halfway through, until golden and crispy. Remove with a slotted spoon and drain on a double thickness of kitchen towel, then stack in a bowl, scrunching over some sea salt.

SERVES 4

READY IN 1 HOUR 10 MINUTES–1 HOUR 25 MINUTES

VEGAN

CELERIAC WEDGES

approximately 1.4kg celeriac, skin cut off, quartered and sliced into wedges 1cm (½in) thick
3 tbsp extra virgin olive oil
sea salt
smoked paprika to season

Celeriac is another low-carb vegetable that will stand in for potatoes. These oven-roasted wedges are more like a roast parsnip, so golden and chewy rather than crisp, and they concentrate in flavour as the moisture is driven off.

1. Preheat the oven to 210°C (fan 190°C/gas mark 6). Arrange the celeriac in a large roasting tin that will hold it in a crowded single layer, drizzle over the olive oil, season with salt and toss to lightly coat it. Roast for 1–1¼ hours, turning with a spatula after 35 minutes. Season with a little paprika.

SERVES 4

READY IN 40 MINUTES

VEGAN

STRAW CELERIAC CAKE

200g maincrop potatoes, peeled
500g celeriac (peeled weight; approximately 750g untrimmed)
sea salt and freshly ground black pepper
4 tbsp vegetable oil, e.g. groundnut

This delicate straw pancake is golden and crispy on the outside and meltingly tender within, based on a French *pommes paillasson* it is another way of making your daily potato allowance go further. It may seem quite deep at the start of the frying but sinks to about half the thickness as it cooks. Just one tip: be sure that your pan really is non-stick. If this is a side for a large meal then it will stretch to serve six.

1. Coarsely grate the potato and celeriac (you can do this with the coarse grating blade of a food processor) and toss them together in a large bowl with some seasoning.

2. Heat a large non-stick frying pan over a medium-low heat, add 2 tablespoons of oil and scatter the potato and celeriac mixture over the base of the pan. Press down with the back of a spoon and cook for about 20 minutes until a uniform deep gold, lifting the cake every now and again to check its progress; you can rotate the frying pan as it cooks if it seems to be colouring evenly.

3. Loosen the cake, and press the mixture down again, then place a non-stick baking tray on top and invert the pan; don't worry if it tears a little, you can reshape it once it's back in the pan. Add the remaining oil to the pan and slip the cake back in. Tidy the sides and fry for another 10 minutes in the same way.

FRYING PAN SUPPERS

THIS CHAPTER TAPS INTO THE SUPPERTIME FIX OF A PAN-FRIED steak, a juicy chop, or fillet of fish, all of which many would miss terribly if the axe came down. And it hasn't quite, but certainly we are going to have to rethink how we serve them to take into account the much smaller quantities recommended to support sustainability. This kind of frying pan supper is my bedrock midweek, and under normal circumstances I would allow a generous 150–200g of protein, with one or two light veggies in tow. To get the scales below 100g per portion, be it fish, chicken or red meat, requires a rethink, or tweaking of the way we approach such suppers.

One ruse is to spread the pleasure by cutting fillets and steaks into strips before frying them up. Alternatively, you can halve the fillets or steaks into thin escalopes, occasionally giving them a bash with a rolling pin, so they cover the same area of the plate as before, while being deliciously delicate to boot. Both these routes sidestep the scenario of a small chunk of meat surrounded by acres of plate that looks like diet rations.

From there it is about rebalancing the protein by serving them with a plethora of veggies, and crucially some pulses, whole grains or nuts, which are key to not feeling hungry afterwards. A mass of low-carb veggies is all very well if you are eating a sizeable steak or chicken fillet, but they will leave you feeling wanting later on in the evening if the portion is small. The other plus to resizing, is that we can indulge in a really good steak, free-range chicken or piece of fish that might previously have seemed indulgently expensive, special occasions aside.

All of these recipes rely on a non-stick frying pan – I get through more of these than I feel comfortable admitting. Nothing cheers me up quite like the luxury of a shiny new pan and the way ingredients skid from one side to other. Small pleasures. But, the good news is they get ever more robust with every replacement, latterly reassuring me the shiny new version will last up to twenty-four times as long as the last one from the same brand. I know from experience that hot fat and stirring alone will wreck the non-stick quality of most pans over time, however careful you are, but, with a bit of luck we are heading towards a pan that could last a lifetime. So do seek out the latest in technology.

And also ensure the brand advertises its pans as being perfluorooctanoic acid (PFOA) free. Until recently PFOA (also known as C8, an industrial surfactant), was used in the production of non-stick linings as an emulsifier, in particular Teflon or polytetrafluoroethylene (PTFE). But it is associated with significant health and environmental concerns – it's a contaminant and resistant to typical environmental degradation processes, so it remains in soil, air and ground water, and is now subject to regulatory action and voluntary phase-outs. Most of the big brands will advertise they are free of these on their websites, but it is worth checking. I would recommend having two pans: one medium 24cm (9½in) pan, which will do for 2 people, and another large 28cm (11in) pan, suitable for 4.

SERVES 4

READY IN 25 MINUTES

FLEXITARIAN

HEALTHY PLANET BURGERS

FOR THE BURGERS

300g lean minced beef
300g cooked green lentils
2 heaped tbsp finely chopped shallots
sea salt and freshly ground black pepper
extra virgin olive oil for frying

TO SERVE

½ red onion, peeled, halved and thinly sliced
8 cocktail gherkins, sliced
4 wholemeal burger buns, halved
English mustard
tomato ketchup
1 beefsteak tomato, sliced

These burgers go down the half-beef, half-lentil route, and they are every bit as satisfying as a pure beef burger. Extras of fried onions, grated cheese, sliced lettuce, or salsa and guacamole for a 'fiesta', are also good. Personally I like to eat these sandwiched between crisp lettuce leaves rather than a bun, but over to you.

1. Place the beef, lentils, shallots and some seasoning in a food processor and whizz to a sticky mixture, so some of the lentils remain whole. Shape the mixture into 8 burgers using a 9cm (3½in) plain round cutter. If you want you can make them in advance, then cover and chill them.

2. Heat 2 teaspoons of oil in a large non-stick frying pan over a medium-low heat and fry the burgers, in batches, for 2 minutes on each side until an even gold, replenishing the oil as necessary. They burn more easily than a pure meat burger, so keep an eye.

3. Combine the sliced onion and gherkins.

4. If serving the burgers with buns, toast the cut side of the buns under a grill, preheated to high. Place a burger on each bun half, smear some mustard over and then plenty of tomato ketchup, or the Mustard mayo (opposite). Next lay over a slice of tomato and season, then scatter over some sliced onion and gherkin.

MUSTARD MAYO

40g mayonnaise
40g soured cream
1 tsp Dijon mustard

Blend all the ingredients in a small bowl, cover and chill until required. This will keep well for several days.

VARIATION

VEGAN BURGERS

SERVES 4

READY IN 35–40 MINUTES

VEGAN

50g coarse bulgur wheat
approximately 3 tbsp extra virgin olive oil
1 aubergine (approximately 250g), cut into 1cm (½in) dice
1 banana shallot, peeled and finely chopped
½ tsp ground allspice
1 tsp ground cumin
½ tsp ground cinnamon
1 x 400g tin black beans, drained and rinsed
1 tbsp lemon juice
sea salt and freshly ground black pepper
3 tbsp finely chopped fresh coriander
50g sesame seeds

These are at their finest sandwiched between a couple of crisp lettuce leaves with some sliced tomato, and soft herbs, such as parsley, coriander and mint leaves, that will add a lively note.

1. Bring a small pan of salted water to the boil and cook the bulgur for 5 minutes to leave it on the chewy side, then drain into a sieve and set aside.

2. Heat 1 tablespoon of oil in a large frying pan over a high heat and fry the aubergine for 6–8 minutes until golden and translucent, stirring frequently, and adding the shallot, spices and 1 teaspoon of oil a couple of minutes before the end.

3. Place this in a food processor with the beans, lemon juice and some seasoning and whizz to a coarse purée. Transfer this mixture to a bowl, and work in the bulgur and coriander. Leave the mixture to cool.

continued overleaf ▶

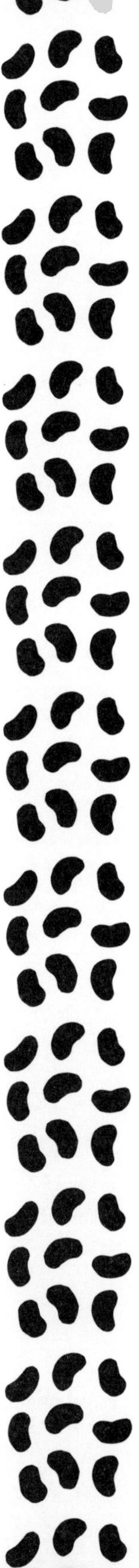

4. Shape the mixture into 4 burgers using an 8cm (3¼in) plain round cutter. Scatter the sesame seeds over a small plate and coat the burgers on each side; you may get a few on the edges but there is no need to coat these thoroughly. Transfer them to a large plate or tray as they are ready. If you chill them in advance of cooking they will firm up – they can be made up to 24 hours in advance.

5. To cook the burgers, heat 1 tablespoon of oil in a large non-stick frying pan over a medium heat and fry for about 3–4 minutes on each side until golden, adding 1 teaspoon of oil to the pan when you turn them.

SERVES 2

READY IN 25–30 MINUTES

FLEXITARIAN

PAPRIKA CHICKEN WITH PECAN AND CORIANDER SALSA

- 2 tbsp extra virgin olive oil
- 1 tbsp lemon juice
- 2 garlic cloves, peeled and crushed to a paste
- ½ tsp paprika
- 150g skinless free-range chicken breast fillet, halved into thin fillets and then cut into thin strips, 5–7cm (½ x 2–2¾in) long
- 100g cherry tomatoes, quartered
- sea salt
- 1 red onion, peeled, halved and thinly sliced
- 2 long red peppers, core and seeds removed, cut into thin strips, 5–7cm (2–2¾in) long
- 125g cooked green lentils
- 25g pecan nuts, finely chopped
- 2 tbsp coarsely chopped fresh coriander
- Greek yoghurt to serve

This is the kind of making a little go a long way that I aspire to, where the chicken is sliced into thin strips and fried, and served with lots of red peppers and onion, and lentils for added protein. While the tomato salsa contributes even more plant protein by way of some nuts.

1. Blend 1 tablespoon of olive oil, the lemon juice, garlic and paprika in a large bowl and stir in the chicken strips.

2. Place the tomatoes in a medium bowl, season with salt and set aside for 15 minutes.

3. Heat 1 tablespoon of oil in a 24cm (9½in) non-stick frying pan over a medium heat and fry the onion and peppers for 7–8 minutes until softened and lightly coloured, stirring frequently.

4. Transfer these to a bowl, add the chicken strips to the pan plus a little of the marinade and stir-fry for about 2 minutes until cooked through. Stir in the lentils and heat through, and return the onions and peppers to the pan.

5. Add the nuts and coriander to the tomatoes. Serve the chicken and peppers with a dollop of Greek yoghurt and the salsa on top.

GET AHEAD

You can marinate the chicken a couple of hours in advance, in which case cover and chill.

SERVES 2

READY IN 20 MINUTES

FLEXITARIAN

MINTY LAMB STEAKS WITH ANCHOVY RAINBOW CHARD

20g fresh mint leaves
approximately 3–4 tbsp extra virgin olive oil
2 tsp balsamic vinegar
1 tsp lemon juice
sea salt and freshly ground black pepper
2 lamb leg steaks (approximately 200g total)
2 anchovy fillets, in oil, drained and sliced
1 garlic clove, peeled and finely chopped
200g young rainbow chard, stalks trimmed, cut into 1cm (½in) thick slices
100g cooked broad beans

One of my favourite ways of roasting lamb is studded with anchovies and garlic, with lashings of mint sauce, all present and correct in this speedy fry-up. The broad beans (fresh or frozen work equally) are an excellent source of plant protein and balance out the restrained size of the steaks. A tomato salad goes very nicely alongside (see Tip).

1. Whizz the mint in a food processor to finely chop it. Scoop it into a small bowl and add 2 tablespoons of oil, the balsamic vinegar, lemon juice and a little salt.

2. Brush the lamb steaks on each side with oil and season them. Heat a 24cm (9½in) non-stick frying pan over a medium-high heat and sear the steaks for 2 minutes on each side to leave them slightly pink in the centre. Transfer them to 2 warm plates and leave to rest for 5–10 minutes while you cook the veggies.

3. Turn the heat down a little, add 2 teaspoons of oil to the pan and briefly fry the anchovies and garlic until fragrant, mashing them into the oil. Pass the chard under a cold tap in a colander. Now add the chard to the pan and stir to coat it, then cover with a lid and cook for 4 minutes, stirring halfway through. If any liquid remains, cook, uncovered, until it evaporates, then stir in the broad beans and heat through.

4. Slice the steak and serve piled on top of the veg, dotted with the sauce (you may not need all of it).

TIP

For the tomato salad, take a selection of different tasty tomatoes, sliced or cut up, sprinkle them with salt and set aside for 15 minutes. Serve with a few slivers of spring onion and a splash of oil if you wish.

GET AHEAD

You can make the mint sauce a couple of hours in advance.

SERVES 6

READY IN 1 HOUR 20 MINUTES

FLEXITARIAN

AUBERGINE-WRAPPED GREEK SAUSAGES WITH ROAST TOMATOES

150g bulgur wheat
1 banana shallot, peeled
1 garlic clove, peeled
1 tsp ground cumin
¼ tsp dried chilli flakes
sea salt and freshly ground black pepper
300g minced lamb
2–3 good-sized aubergines, trimmed
extra virgin olive oil for brushing and drizzling
500g small cherry tomatoes, e.g. baby plum, halved
3 tbsp fresh oregano leaves

These lamb and bulgur wheat sausages are wrapped in slices of fried aubergine before being baked with cherry tomatoes. For the veg lover they are infinitely preferable to a line-up of pure pork sausages; you also have a healthy range of nutrients including two of your veg a day and some whole grains. But a salad and some wholemeal pittas for mopping up those juices will spin them out even further.

1. Soak the bulgur wheat in cold water for 5 minutes. To make the sausages, whizz the shallot, garlic, cumin, chilli and some salt in a food processor. Drain and add the bulgur and lamb, and whizz to a sticky paste. If you want to check the seasoning, then fry a smidgeon of the mixture in a frying pan.

2. Taking a heaped tablespoon of the mixture at a time, form into 12 spindle-shaped sausages about 8–9cm (3¼–3½ in) long. Heat a large non-stick frying pan over a medium heat and colour these in batches (no need for oil) on about three sides, then set aside.

3. Preheat the oven to 220°C (fan 200°C/gas mark 7). Cut each aubergine lengthways, into 1cm (½in) thick slices, to give you 12 slices in total (not including the end slices – reserve these for some other use; see Tip).

4. Heat a clean large non-stick frying pan over a high heat, brush as many aubergine slices as will fit in a single layer with oil on one side, and season. Fry oiled-side down for 1½–2 minutes until golden, then brush the topside with oil and fry likewise. They don't need to be fully cooked through, just coloured. Remove and cook the remainder in the same fashion.

5. Starting at the rounded end of each aubergine slice roll up a sausage, skewer with a cocktail stick and arrange in a large roasting tin with a little space in between. Toss the tomatoes with 2 tablespoons of oregano leaves, some seasoning and a tablespoon of oil and scatter over and between the rolls.

6. Scatter over the remaining oregano, drizzle over a little more oil and bake for 30–35 minutes until everything is nice and golden.

TIP

Any excess aubergine can be diced and fried up in olive oil with a little seasoning, to eat like a roast vegetable.

SERVES 4

READY IN 20 MINUTES

VEGAN

QUINOA AND SUGAR SNAP STIR-FRY

- 2 avocados, halved and pitted
- 1 generous tbsp lemon juice
- sea salt and freshly ground black pepper
- 1 tbsp extra virgin olive oil
- 2 red onions, peeled and chopped
- 150g sugar snaps, ends trimmed and cut into 1cm (½in) dice
- ½ tsp ground allspice
- ½ tsp ground cinnamon
- 1 x 250g packet cooked quinoa
- 40g rocket, coarsely chopped
- 40g watercress, coarsely chopped

TO SERVE

- finely chopped roasted hazelnuts
- chopped fresh flat-leaf parsley

This stir-fry is a talented all-rounder, vegan as is, it draws from quinoa, sugar snaps, hazelnuts and avocados as different sources of protein. Hungry vegans might like to add more quinoa, while flexitarians could broaden it out with a poached egg (see page 81) or some thin medallions of pork fillet or lamb. I always like to have a packet or two of pre-cooked quinoa and other grains in the cupboard (as well as packets of dried), for this kind of super-whizzy scenario.

1. Whizz the avocado flesh, lemon juice and some seasoning in a food processor until smooth.

2. Heat the oil in a large 28cm (11in) non-stick frying pan over a medium heat and fry the onion for about 8 minutes until softened and lightly coloured, adding the sugar snaps and spices a minute or so before the end.

3. Stir in the quinoa, season and fry for a couple of minutes to heat through, then stir in the rocket and watercress and fold over a few times so it relaxes.

4. Serve the stir-fry dolloped with the avocado purée, scattered with hazelnuts and parsley.

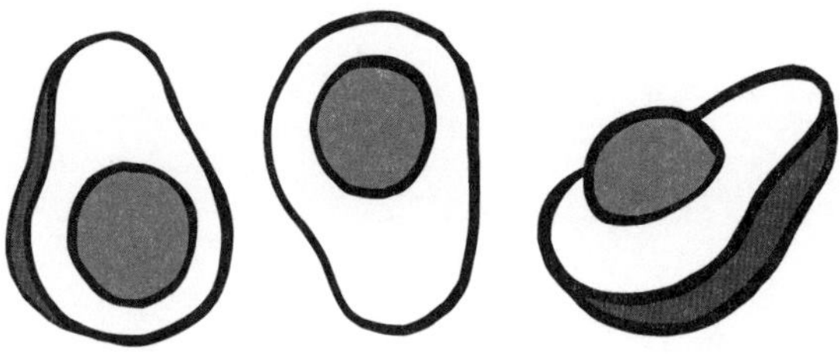

SERVES 2

READY IN 20–25 MINUTES

FLEXITARIAN

HEALTHY PLANET STEAK AND MASH

- 1 x 400g tin borlotti beans, drained and rinsed
- 2 tbsp lemon juice
- approximately 2 tbsp extra virgin olive oil, plus extra for drizzling
- sea salt and freshly ground black pepper
- 2 x 100g lean sirloin steaks
- 1 banana shallot, peeled and finely chopped
- 100g wild mushrooms, e.g. *pied de mouton*, trimmed and sliced
- 150–200g chicory heads (trimmed weight, approximately 2), halved lengthways and sliced
- 1 handful of coarsely chopped fresh flat-leaf parsley

Minute steaks are a win-win, half the meat of a big steak, so not only more affordable but planet-friendly and cooked in a jiffy. This borlotti mash joins those in the Beyond potatoes chapter (see page 147) and can be served with any of the stews or small cuts, to turn them into a more substantial dish.

1. Whizz the beans with the lemon juice, 1 tablespoon of oil and some seasoning in a food processor until smooth.

2. Place the steaks between two sheets of clingfilm and pound with a rolling pin to a thickness of 1cm (½in). Brush them with oil and season on each side. Heat a 24cm (9½in) non-stick frying pan over a medium-high heat and sear the steaks for 1 minute on each side. Transfer these to 2 warm plates and leave to rest for about 10 minutes while you cook the veg.

3. Add 1 tablespoon of oil to the pan, stir the shallot into the oil, then add the mushrooms and fry for a few minutes until softened and starting to colour, cooking off any liquid that is given out. Add the chicory and fry for a few minutes longer, then season and stir in the parsley. Spoon this beside the steaks, then gently heat the bean mash in the pan and serve drizzled with a little more oil.

continued overleaf ▶

VARIATION

VEGAN 'STEAKS'

SERVES 4

READY IN 35 MINUTES

VEGAN

125g pearled spelt
8 medium flat-cap mushrooms
4 garlic cloves, peeled and finely chopped
5 tbsp extra virgin olive oil
sea salt and freshly ground black pepper
2 banana shallots, peeled and finely chopped
150g button mushrooms, stalks trimmed and thinly sliced
finely grated zest of 1 lemon, plus 1 tablespoon of juice
2 tbsp coarsely chopped fresh flat-leaf parsley
2 tbsp chopped fresh dill
30g roasted and chopped hazelnuts to serve

Big cupped mushrooms are my vegetarian stand-in for steak, but they need a little bolstering to ensure satiety, and here I've stuffed them with spelt. Serve with the borlotti mash on page 177. Don't forget to make up double the amount of mash as this serves 4. You can either use portobello or the large floppy flat-cap mushrooms, which provide a base for the spelt and mushroom pilaf.

1. Bring a medium pan of salted water to the boil, add the spelt and simmer for 17–20 minutes until tender, then drain into a sieve.

2. At the same time preheat the oven to 200°C (fan 180°C/gas mark 6). Trim the mushroom stalks level with the cup and arrange them in one or two roasting tins cup-side up. Divide the garlic between the cups, drizzle over 3 tablespoons of olive oil, season and bake for 25 minutes.

3. Five minutes before the mushrooms come out of the oven, heat the remaining oil in a large non-stick frying pan over a medium heat and fry the shallots for a couple of minutes until softened and just starting to colour, stirring frequently. Add the button mushrooms, season and continue to fry for several minutes until lightly coloured. Stir in the spelt and lemon zest and heat through. Stir in the herbs and lemon juice and taste for seasoning.

4. Divide this between the mushrooms, and scatter over some hazelnuts. These are good eaten both hot or warm.

SERVES 4

READY IN 1 HOUR–
1 HOUR 10 MINUTES

PESCATARIAN

SESAME MACKEREL WITH ORANGE AND BEETROOT SALAD

75g wheat berries
2 oranges
1 tbsp balsamic vinegar
sea salt and freshly ground black pepper
approximately 5 tbsp extra virgin olive oil
3 cooked and peeled beetroot (unvinegared), cut into 1cm (½in) dice
2 tbsp finely chopped fresh dill, plus a little extra to serve
2 x 180g packets mackerel (4 fillets)
2 tsp Dijon mustard
50g sesame seeds
4 handfuls of watercress

Mackerel fillets are one of the best sources of the long-chain omega-3 fats EPA and DHA. Here the mackerel is married with a range of other nutritious ingredients – orange, beetroot, watercress, sesame seeds and olive oil, plus wheat berries which are arguably my favourite whole grain. This salad is also lovely with simply fried salmon (see Crispy salmon with freekeh and cavolo on page 185).

1. Bring a medium pan of water to the boil, add the wheat berries and simmer for 50–60 minutes until tender, then drain into a sieve and leave to cool.

2. To make the salad, cut the skin and pith off the oranges and run a small sharp knife between the segments to remove them, dropping them into a medium bowl. Whisk the balsamic vinegar with a little salt and pepper in another medium bowl, add 4 tablespoons of olive oil, then stir in the beetroot and the dill. You can prepare the recipe to this point a couple of hours in advance.

3. To prepare the mackerel, score the skin diagonally in a couple of places, then brush the skin with the mustard. Spread the sesame seeds on a plate and dip the skin to lightly coat it. Set aside on a plate.

4. To cook the fish, heat 2 teaspoons of oil in a large non-stick frying pan over a medium heat. Fry the mackerel fillets half at a time. Place them skin-side down and cook for 2 minutes until the sesame seeds are golden, then turn and cook for another 2 minutes. Transfer to a plate, scrape out the pan, refresh the oil and cook the remainder in the same way.

5. To serve, place a mackerel fillet skin-side up on four plates. Place a pile of watercress to the side, mix in the orange segments. Add the wheat berries to the beetroot and spoon over the fish and salad, and scatter over a little more dill.

VEGETARIAN AND VEGAN SWAPS

For a vegetarian supper, leave out the mackerel, mix 100g crumbled feta into the beetroot salad, and scatter over 80g chopped walnuts or pecans.

For a vegan supper, leave out the mackerel and serve the salad with the Cucumber and edamame salsa (see page 183).

SERVES 2

READY IN 20 MINUTES

PESCATARIAN

MACKEREL WITH WALNUT DRESSING

25g walnuts
1 tsp balsamic vinegar
sea salt and freshly ground black pepper
approximately 3 tbsp extra virgin olive oil
2 fennel bulbs, green shoots and tough outer sheath discarded, halved and thinly sliced
¼ eating apple, cored and thinly sliced
100g cooked freekeh or spelt (see Tip)
2 x 100g mackerel fillets, skin scored diagonally at 3cm (1¼in) intervals
a little finely chopped fresh dill
2 handfuls of lamb's lettuce

Singing with goodness – omega-3 oil in the mackerel, a smattering of walnuts and whole grains, a superfood fry-up.

1. Pound the walnuts in a pestle and mortar to coarse crumbs, stir in the balsamic vinegar, season and add 1 tablespoon of oil.

2. Heat 1 tablespoon of oil in a 24cm (9½in) non-stick frying pan over a medium heat and fry the fennel and apple for 5–7 minutes until softened and lightly coloured, then stir in the freekeh or spelt, season and heat through. Divide this between 2 warm plates.

3. Brush the mackerel with oil on each side and season. Sear, skin down, for 3 minutes, then turn and cook for 30 seconds. Scatter a little dill over the fennel, place the mackerel on top, then a pile of lamb's lettuce and dollop with the walnut dressing.

TIP

Any cooked whole grain can be included here.

SERVES 4

READY IN 45 MINUTES

PESCATARIAN

SEARED TUNA WITH CUCUMBER AND EDAMAME SALSA

FOR THE SALSA

- **1 cucumber, ends discarded, halved lengthways and cut into 1cm (½in) strips**
- **sea salt and freshly ground black pepper**
- **2 tbsp currants**
- **50ml cider vinegar**
- **50g caster sugar**
- **150g frozen soya (edamame) beans**
- **4 tbsp extra virgin olive oil, plus extra for brushing**
- **2 tsp grainy mustard**
- **2 tbsp finely chopped shallots**
- **2 tbsp small capers (*nonpareille*), rinsed**
- **2 tbsp finely chopped fresh dill (see Tip)**
- **2 tbsp snipped fresh chives**

FOR THE TUNA

- **4 x 100g yellowfin tuna steaks, 2–3cm (¾–1¼in) thick**
- **⅓ tsp finely grated lemon zest, plus a squeeze of juice**
- **rocket leaves to serve**

This little salsa involves my go-to of lightly pickled cucumber, fab with a Nordic nod to mustard, dill and chives. It is as much salad as salsa, so ladle it on. Tuna steaks are one of my convenience mid-week standbys. I like to have a pack or two of fillets in the freezer, that only take a couple of hours to defrost, and are guaranteed to be 'fresher' than the fish counter.

1. For the salsa, slice the cucumber into 3mm (⅛in) pieces. Season the cucumber with salt in a large bowl and set aside for 30 minutes before rinsing in a colander and returning to a large, clean bowl. Mix in the currants. Bring 50 ml water and the vinegar to the boil with the sugar in a small saucepan, pour over the cucumber and currants and leave to cool, then drain into a sieve and dry on a double thickness of kitchen towel.

2. Meanwhile bring a pan of water to the boil and cook the beans according to the packet instructions, then drain into a sieve and leave to cool.

3. Combine 3 tablespoons of oil, the mustard, shallots, capers and herbs in a medium serving bowl, then stir in the pickled cucumber and beans, and season. Cover and chill until required, it will keep well for at least half a day.

4. For the tuna, heat a large non-stick frying pan over a medium-high heat, brush the tuna steaks each side with oil, and season. Sear for about 2 minutes on each side,

continued overleaf ▶

leaving them with a slight give to ensure they remain moist – there should be no visible red at the sides.

5. Blend the remaining tablespoon of oil, the lemon zest and juice in a small bowl and toss with the rocket and a pinch of salt.

6. Serve the tuna with the salsa spooned on top and around, and a pile of rocket.

TIP

The herbs are open to variation, both coriander and fresh flat-leaf parsley can be used too.

VEGAN SWAP

For a vegan supper, leave out the tuna and serve the salsa with the Orange and beetroot salad *(see page 180).*

SERVES 4

READY IN 20–25 MINUTES

PESCATARIAN

CRISPY SALMON WITH FREEKEH AND CAVOLO

FOR THE DRESSING

2 tsp pomegranate molasses
1 tsp Dijon mustard
1 tsp finely grated fresh root ginger
sea salt
2 tbsp extra virgin olive oil

FOR THE SALMON AND VEGETABLES

50g freekeh
350–400g cavolo nero, stalks discarded, leaves thickly sliced
4 x 100g skinless salmon fillets
1 tsp extra virgin olive oil

TO SERVE

2 spring onions, trimmed and thinly sliced
coarsely chopped fresh coriander
fine slivers of medium-hot red chilli

Just a whisper of freekeh provides a satisfying hit of whole grains, without being too heavy. And, like most grains, it comes to life in the presence of jazzy flavours, here a little ginger and pomegranate in the dressing. This is still on fine form when it has cooled, so definitely worth cooking up extra with lunch the day after in mind.

1. Whisk the pomegranate molasses, mustard, ginger and a little salt together in a small bowl, then gradually whisk in the oil to a thick emulsion and add 1–2 teaspoons of water to thin the dressing to a trickling consistency.

2. Bring a medium pan of salted water to the boil. Add the freekeh and simmer for 15 minutes or until just tender, then drain into a colander.

3. Meanwhile, bring a large pan of salted water to the boil, add the cavolo nero and simmer for 4–5 minutes or until tender, then drain into a sieve and press out the excess liquid using the back of a large spoon.

4. Heat a large non-stick frying pan over a medium heat, season the salmon with salt on the topside and fry this side for about 5 minutes until golden and crispy and you can see the fillets have cooked through by a third to half, then turn and cook the other side for about 3 minutes – exact timings will depend on the thickness of the fillets – they should have just lost their translucency in the centre.

continued overleaf ▶

5. Heat 1 teaspoon of oil in medium frying pan over a medium heat and stir-fry the freekeh for a minute or two to warm through.

6. Arrange the cavolo nero and freekeh together to the side of the salmon, spoon the dressing over all three, then scatter with the spring onions, coriander and chilli.

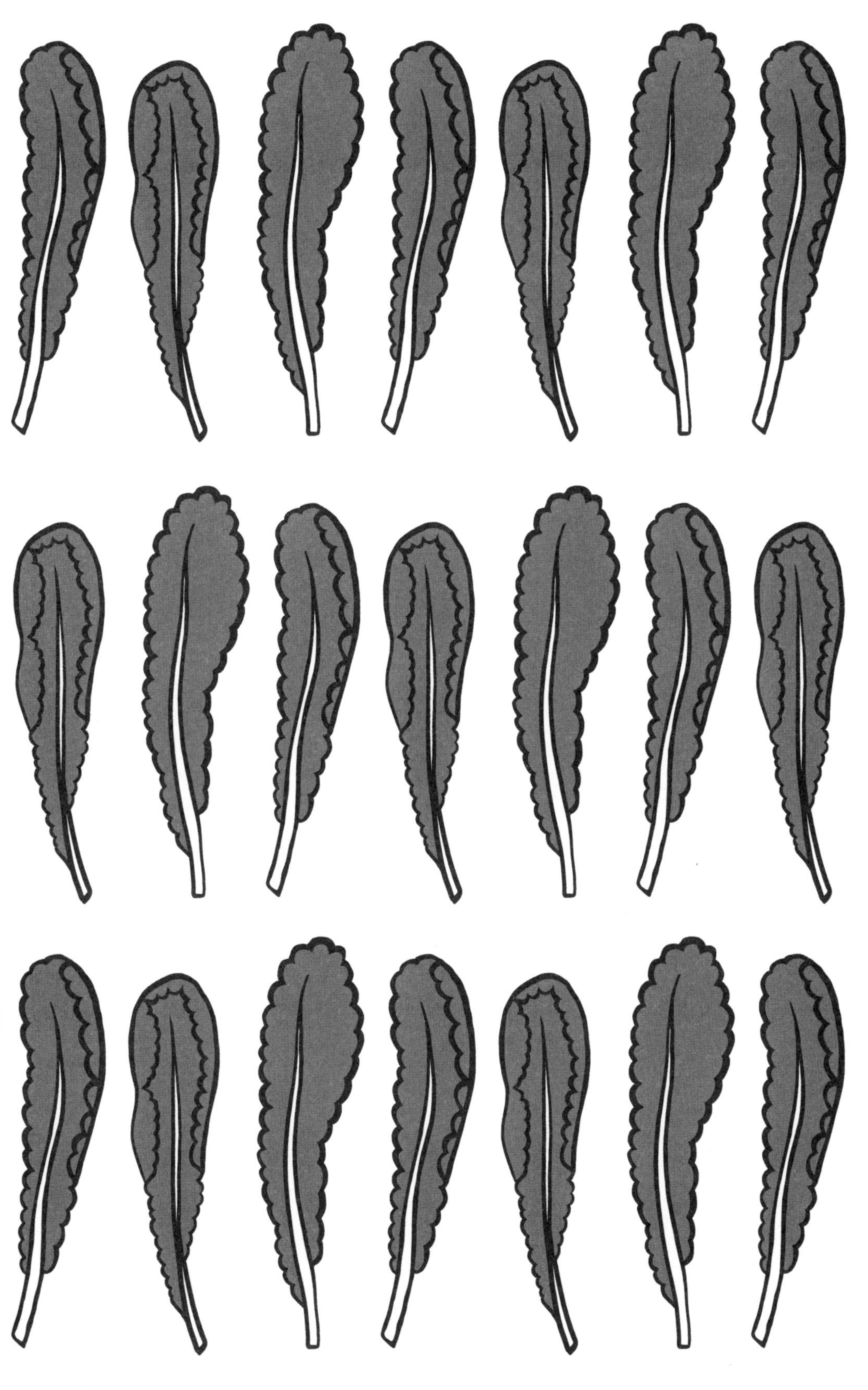

SERVES 4

READY IN 20–25 MINUTES

PESCATARIAN

SEABASS FISH FINGERS WITH TARTARE SAUCE

FOR THE TARTARE SAUCE

100g mayonnaise
50g soured cream
1 tbsp finely chopped small capers (*nonpareille*), plus a few extra to serve
1 tbsp finely chopped cocktail gherkins
1 heaped tbsp finely chopped fresh flat-leaf parsley, plus extra to serve

FOR THE FISH FINGERS

1 medium free-range egg
75ml skimmed milk
sea salt and freshly ground black pepper
60g wholemeal spelt flour
1 tsp baking powder
vegetable oil for shallow frying, e.g. groundnut
2 x 100g skin-on seabass fillets, halved lengthways into strips
125g button mushrooms, stalks trimmed (see Tip) and halved downwards

Fish fingers made with the luxury of seabass and a homemade tartare sauce is on my list to be eating when the ship goes down. Here I've cut the amount of fish I would normally use by serving the goujons half and half with some fried mushrooms – equally good with tartare sauce. Both can be turned into a suitably indulgent warm sandwich using wholemeal pittas (see Tips for the table).

1. Combine the ingredients for the tartare sauce in a bowl. Cover and set aside.

2. If using a blender, place the egg, milk and a pinch of salt in a blender, then add the flour and baking powder and whizz until smooth. Scrape down any flour clinging to the sides and whizz again. Or, if making by hand, whisk the egg in a small bowl, then sift and stir in the flour and baking powder, add the salt and mix to a lumpy dough. Gradually whisk in the milk until smooth.

3. Season the batter well in a medium bowl. Heat the vegetable oil to a depth of 1cm (½in) in a large frying pan, over a medium heat. Once a drop of batter sizzles in the oil, dip the fish fillets in the bowl of batter and shallow fry for about 4 minutes in total, until golden and crispy on each side. If necessary, cook them in batches so as not to overcrowd the pan. Remove the fish fingers with a slotted spoon, then drain them on a double thickness of kitchen towel.

4. Now repeat with the mushrooms: stir them into the remaining batter to coat them, and shallow fry for a few minutes, until golden and crisp. Remove them from the pan with a slotted spoon. Serve with tartare sauce, scattered with extra capers and parsley.

TIP

The trimmed mushroom stalks can be put aside and used to make vegetable stock.

GET AHEAD

The sauce can be prepared a day in advance, in which case cover and chill.

TIPS FOR THE TABLE

For a treat of a sandwich, fill warm wholemeal pittas with shredded lettuce, the fish fingers, mushrooms and tartare sauce.

SERVES 4

READY IN 20–25 MINUTES

PESCATARIAN

SALMON WITH SPINACH AND CHICKPEAS

approximately 3 tbsp extra virgin olive oil
25g pine nuts
25g currants
500g spinach
½ tsp ground cumin
small pinch of saffron threads (optional)
1 x 400g tin chickpeas, drained and rinsed
sea salt and freshly ground black pepper
400g skinless salmon fillets, cut across into 1cm (½in) strips, 7–10cm (2¾–4in) long
lemon wedges to serve

Anyone who has ever visited Seville will know that *espinacas con garbanzos* is one of the very finest tapas to be enjoyed with a small glass of sherry. Adding some buttery slivers of salmon into the equation sends it to the next tier.

1. Heat 1 teaspoon of oil in a 28cm (11in) non-stick frying pan over a medium-high heat and stir-fry the pine nuts and currants until the nuts are lightly golden, then transfer them to a small bowl.

2. Add another teaspoon of oil to the pan and fry about a third of the spinach until it wilts. Transfer this to a large bowl and cook the remainder in the same way.

3. Add 1 tablespoon of oil to the pan, and stir in the cumin, and saffron if including, and then the chickpeas, season and stir-fry to heat through. Mix these into the spinach.

4. Spread the salmon strips over a plate and season them on one side. Lay half of these over the base of the frying pan (without adding more oil) and sear for about 1 minute on the first side and 30 seconds on the second until lightly coloured and cooked through, then remove to a plate and cook the remainder.

5. Serve the spinach with the salmon strips on top, scattered with the pine nuts and currants, accompanied by lemon wedges.

VEGETARIAN AND VEGAN SWAPS

This salad is lovely on its own as a vegan main, simply omit the salmon and allow this for two people. Vegetarians can serve a poached or fried egg *(see page 81)* *in addition.*

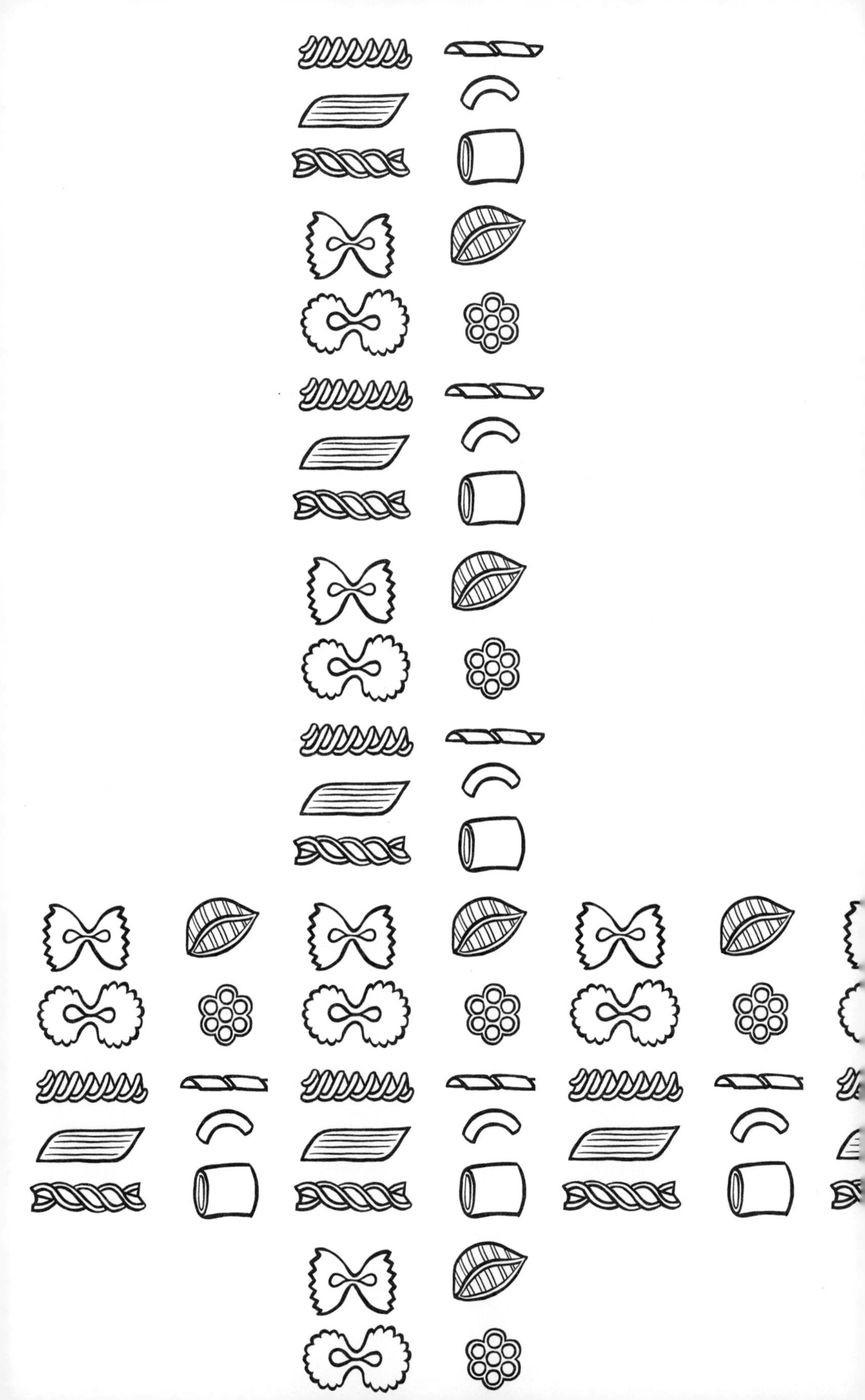

PASTA AND PILAFS

THIS CHAPTER IS PRINCIPALLY DEDICATED TO WHOLE GRAINS IN their sweeping variety. If the greatest challenge for flexitarians has to do with radically reducing our consumption of animal protein, an equally great challenge common to nearly everyone of differing dietary persuasions is how we can increase our intake of whole grains to over 230g a day (dried weight), so they account for up to 60 per cent of our energy. For the average person, this is a big ask. Hands up who can tick the box, I know I can't.

But taking a stroll down the sunny side of the street, in relation to choice and how we can go about eating whole grains, we've never had it better. If I look back to my own childhood, when 'whole grain' was synonymous with gritty cereal pellets and sliced brown bread, the grain scene today has evolved beyond recognition. Most of this, ironically, has been driven by our appetite for new but ancient grains (and pseudo grains) that have been around for millennia, such as spelt, quinoa, buckwheat, red, black and wild rice, millet, amaranth and teff. Today these find their way into bread, pasta and snacks, and we have also learnt to include the whole grains in many ways beyond the obvious. Whether that is to use them differently, such as including just a few in a salad of leaves or roast vegetables, or for instance, adding a smattering to an omelette mix (see page 62) or making a porridge with them, the incentives for eating more are rich and diverse. And in keeping with this, their image has evolved from being frumpy to fashionable.

So, a part of this chapter is about using whole grains in their whole form to make lovely pilafs and risottos, and the other half is about pastas that look beyond refined wheat. Two years ago I remember writing about pasta made with legumes, black bean and edamame bean spaghetti, slightly nervous that they were so niche and new that they might sink without trace, but instead they have been joined by pastas made from any number of whole grains – quinoa, spelt, buckwheat, and legumes such as chickpeas, as well as green peas and lentils. A lot of this has been driven by small producers dedicated to pushing an agenda of good nutrition with exciting products that meet our needs, but when the big commercial producers start making such pastas, then you know that the revolution is in full swing.

SERVES 4

READY IN 1 HOUR 30 MINUTES

FLEXITARIAN

LAMB PILAF WITH WATERMELON-AND-LEMON RELISH

FOR THE PILAF

3 tbsp extra virgin olive oil
400g lamb fillet, cut into 2cm (¾in) thick slices
800ml chicken stock
sea salt and freshly ground black pepper
250g frozen baby broad beans
1 white or yellow onion, peeled, halved and sliced
2 garlic cloves, peeled and finely chopped
½ tsp ground cumin
½ tsp ground allspice
225g bulgur wheat, rinsed in a sieve
1 tbsp fresh lemon thyme leaves
2 strips of orange zest (removed with a potato peeler)
150ml white wine
6 tbsp coarsely chopped fresh coriander

FOR THE RELISH

150g seeded watermelon, cut into 1cm (½in) dice
1 tbsp finely chopped preserved lemon

Dished up with the jazzy touch of a watermelon and preserved lemon relish, a cucumber and yoghurt dip and some pumpkin seeds, there is little chance of this spicy bulgur wheat pilaf appearing frumpy. In fact it is worth taking these extras on board, as a blueprint for dressing up any grain dish. This particular pilaf also makes excellent party material, given that you can up the numbers with ease.

1. Heat 1 tablespoon of olive oil in a medium saucepan over a medium-high heat and colour the lamb slices on each side, in batches so as not to overcrowd the pan. Return all the lamb to the pan, add 500ml stock and some seasoning, bring to the boil then cover and cook over a gentle heat for 1 hour until tender. Strain off and discard the liquid.

2. At the same time, bring a medium pan of water to the boil and simmer the broad beans for about 5 minutes until tender, then drain them into a sieve.

3. Heat 1 tablespoon of oil in a large saucepan over a medium heat and fry the onion for 5–7 minutes until golden, stirring frequently, and adding the garlic and ground spices just before the end.

4. Stir in the bulgur wheat, and add the thyme, orange zest and some seasoning. Add the remaining 300ml stock and the wine, bring the liquid to the boil, cover with a tight-fitting lid and cook over a low heat for 5 minutes,

TO SERVE

pumpkin seeds
cacik (see below)

then add the lamb and broad beans and cook, covered, for another 5 minutes.

5. Without removing the lid, remove from the heat and leave the pilaf for 15 minutes, during which time it will dry out further and become more tender.

6. Combine the watermelon, preserved lemon and remaining tablespoon of olive oil in a bowl. Stir the coriander into the pilaf and remove the orange zest.

7. Serve with the watermelon relish, scattered with pumpkin seeds, accompanied by cacik.

CACIK

SERVES 6
READY IN 10 MINUTES
VEGETARIAN

500g full-fat Greek or enriched yoghurt (see introduction)
1 small garlic clove, peeled and crushed to a paste
sea salt
1 cucumber, ends discarded, peeled and coarsely grated
2 heaped tbsp finely chopped dill or chives, plus a little snipped to serve
extra virgin olive oil
cayenne pepper for dusting

This Turkish take on tzatziki has me in its thrall, there is something about the fine strands of grated cucumber coated in yoghurt that is heart-stoppingly good, and it's a doddle to make. Great fridge dipping material too. You either want a full-fat Greek yoghurt here, or you could enrich a lower fat Greek yoghurt with a tablespoon of soured cream.

1. Spoon the yoghurt into a large bowl and blend in the garlic and a little salt. Using your hands squeeze out as much of the liquid from the cucumber as possible, then stir this into the yoghurt with the dill or chives.

2. Transfer to a serving bowl and drizzle over some olive oil, dust with cayenne and scatter with a little snipped dill or chives.

SERVES 4

READY IN 25–30 MINUTES

PESCATARIAN

ASPARAGUS SPELTOTTO WITH CRAB

- 100g pearled spelt
- 300g fine asparagus, ends trimmed
- 3 tbsp extra virgin olive oil
- 300g trimmed leeks, halved lengthways and thinly sliced
- 1 garlic clove, peeled and finely chopped
- 100ml white wine
- 2 tbsp chia seeds
- finely grated zest of 1 lemon, plus 1 tbsp juice
- 500ml vegetable stock
- sea salt and freshly ground black pepper
- 10g unsalted butter
- 200g brown and white crab meat

This speltotto is light and soupy compared to its rich and buttery Italian cousin, risotto. Spelt takes the place of rice, and chia seeds add in a little plant protein, while the crab provides the high-end glamour.

1. Bring a small pan of salted water to the boil, add the spelt and simmer for 20 minutes or until just tender. Drain into a sieve and set aside.

2. Meanwhile, cut off and reserve the asparagus tips, and finely slice the stalks. Heat 2 tablespoons of olive oil in a large saucepan and fry the leek and garlic for about 5 minutes until softened and glossy, without colouring, stirring occasionally. Stir in the sliced asparagus, add the wine and simmer to reduce by half. Stir in the chia seeds and the lemon zest, add the stock and some seasoning, bring to the boil and simmer for 5–8 minutes until the vegetables are tender. Stir in the spelt and taste for seasoning.

3. While the risotto base is cooking, bring a small pan of salted water to the boil, add the asparagus tips and simmer for 3–4 minutes or until just tender. Drain into a sieve, return to the pan and toss with the butter.

4. Dress the crab with 1 tablespoon each of olive oil and lemon juice and lightly season.

5. Serve the risotto in bowls with the crab spooned on top, and the asparagus tips scattered over.

SERVES 4

READY IN 20–25 MINUTES

VEGETARIAN

SPEEDY CAULIFLOWER, LENTIL AND WATERCRESS RISOTTO

600–700g cauliflower florets
2 tbsp extra virgin olive oil, plus extra to serve
2 large banana shallots, peeled and finely chopped
½ celery heart, trimmed, thinly sliced and then chopped
2 garlic cloves, peeled and finely chopped
150ml dry vermouth or vegetarian white wine
approximately 300ml vegetable stock
1 x 250g packet cooked green lentils
sea salt and freshly ground black pepper
freshly grated nutmeg to season
10g unsalted butter
50g grated vegetarian Parmesan-style cheese, plus extra to serve
80–100g watercress, coarsely chopped
1 large handful of coarsely chopped fresh flat-leaf parsley, plus extra to serve

This is as much soup as risotto, a clean and lean take on the genre, where cauliflower and lentils take the place of a grain. Not only fast, it is also low in carbs, which does it for me, you don't even suffer guilt in the aftermath.

1. Whizz the cauliflower in batches in a food processor to finely chop to 'rice'. Heat 2 tablespoons of olive oil in a large saucepan over a medium heat and fry the shallots and celery for several minutes until glossy and softened.

2. Stir in the garlic and fry a minute longer, then add the cauliflower and stir-fry for another 3 minutes.

3. Add the vermouth or wine, turn the heat up and cook until this evaporates.

4. Add 300ml stock, bring to the boil and simmer over a low heat for 3–5 minutes until tender, then stir in the lentils to heat through. Season with salt, pepper and nutmeg, stir in the butter, cheese, watercress and parsley. You can add a little more stock if you want it soupier.

5. Serve in shallow bowls scattered with more parsley and cheese, and a drizzle of oil.

SERVES 4

READY IN 25–30 MINUTES

VEGETARIAN

SPINACH AND MILLET PORRIDGE WITH CASHEWS

FOR THE PORRIDGE

150g millet
500g spinach
2 tbsp extra virgin olive oil
10g unsalted butter
3 banana shallots, peeled, halved and thinly sliced
1 celery heart, trimmed and thinly sliced
3 garlic cloves, peeled and finely sliced
¼ tsp ground allspice
¼ tsp ground cinnamon
125ml vegetarian white wine
sea salt and freshly ground black pepper
freshly grated nutmeg to season
ground sumac for dusting
4 tbsp roasted cashews, coarsely crushed

FOR THE MINT YOGHURT

2 tsp finely chopped fresh mint
1 tsp lemon juice
150g full-fat Greek yoghurt

I love the idea of savoury porridge, something that is just beginning to enter our lexicon even though it is a staple of many an African country. And millet is the perfect foundation, though I trod rather gingerly around this tiny ochre grain when I started cooking with it, before realizing that my hesitance was to do with its glutinous texture. Millet has a distinctive flavour and alluring bitterness, but it benefits from shedding some of the starch that otherwise results in a gloopy finish. Cooking it before using it to make a porridge ensures a creamy but firm grain.

1. Bring a medium pan of water to the boil, add the millet, and simmer for 15 minutes until just tender, skimming off any foam that rises to the surface in the first few minutes, and stirring regularly to ensure it doesn't stick. Drain into a sieve and rinse under the cold tap to rid it of all the starch.

2. Meanwhile, pass the spinach under a cold tap in a colander, then place the spinach in a large saucepan. Cover with a lid and steam over a gentle heat for 10 minutes or until it collapses, stirring halfway through. Tip it into the colander and press out the excess water using a potato masher or the back of a ladle. Coarsely chop it on a board.

3. At the same time heat the oil and butter in another medium-large saucepan over a low heat and fry the shallots and celery for about 15 minutes until golden, stirring occasionally and adding the garlic, allspice and cinnamon a couple of minutes before the end. Add the wine and simmer until well-reduced and syrupy.

4. Stir the millet into the vegetable base, and then the spinach. Season with salt, pepper and nutmeg and heat through.

5. While the porridge is cooking, combine the ingredients for the yoghurt in a small bowl and season with salt.

6. Serve the porridge dolloped with the yoghurt, dusted with sumac and scattered with the nuts.

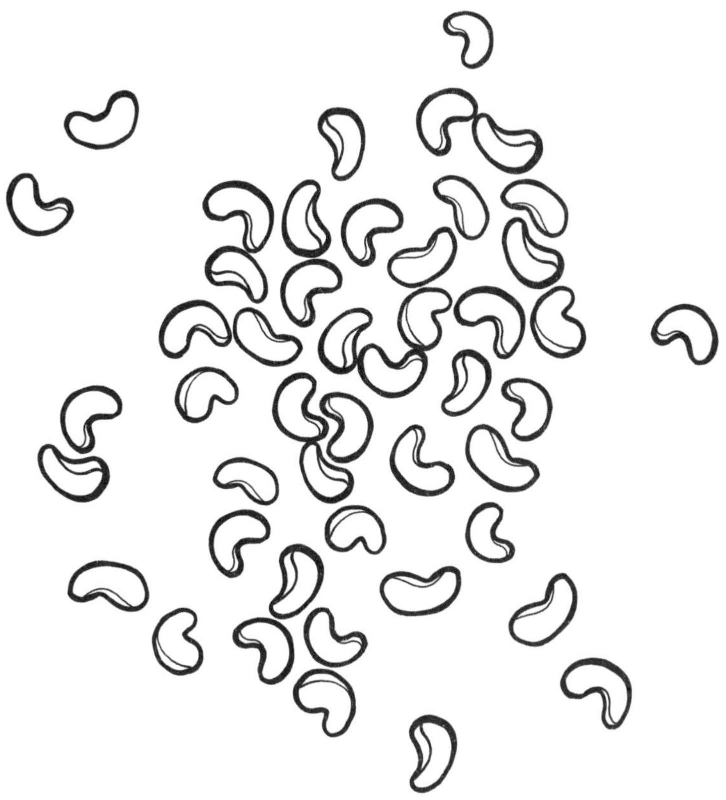

SERVES 6

READY IN 40 MINUTES

VEGAN

BULGUR WHEAT, CASHEW NUT AND ROCKET PILAF

- 3 tbsp extra virgin olive oil
- 1 large white or yellow onion, peeled and chopped
- 1 tsp ground cumin
- 1 tsp ground coriander
- pinch of dried chilli flakes
- 3 garlic cloves, peeled and finely chopped
- 3 strips of lemon zest (removed with a potato peeler)
- 1 tbsp thyme leaves
- 1 bay leaf
- 350g bulgur wheat
- 150ml vegan white wine
- 500ml vegetable stock
- sea salt
- 180g rocket, roughly chopped
- 125g roasted cashews
- coconut yoghurt to serve (or, for non-vegans, soured cream)

This is slightly more evolved than the sides in Beyond potatoes (see page 147), a smattering more flavourings, some rocket and plenty of nuts that add in extra protein. It's lovely dished up with a spicy chutney, balsamic onions, a Red pepper confit (see page 99) or Cacik (see page 197), a cucumber and yoghurt relish.

1. Heat the olive oil in a medium saucepan over a medium heat, add the onion and fry for 5–8 minutes until lightly coloured, stirring occasionally. Add the spices, garlic, lemon and herbs, give everything a stir and cook for a moment longer.

2. Add the bulgur wheat and give it a stir, then add the wine, stock and some salt, bring to the boil and simmer over a low heat for 8 minutes.

3. Remove from the heat, cover and leave to stand for 20 minutes. Remove the bay leaf and lemon zest, add the rocket and cashews and toss.

4. Serve with coconut yoghurt or soured cream.

SERVES 4

READY IN 1 HOUR

FLEXITARIAN

TOMATO AND CHICKEN SPELT WITH BASIL AND PISTACHIO PESTO

FOR THE PILAF

- **3 tbsp extra virgin olive oil**
- **3 banana shallots, peeled, halved lengthways and thinly sliced**
- **2 long red peppers, core and seeds discarded, thickly sliced across**
- **1 heaped tsp ground coriander**
- **1 heaped tsp ground cumin**
- **300g pearled spelt**
- **650ml chicken or vegetable stock**
- **1 cinnamon stick**
- **sea salt and freshly ground black pepper**
- **200g cherry tomatoes, halved or quartered**
- **300g free-range chicken thighs, skinned and boned, or skinless chicken thigh fillets, cut into 2–3cm (¾–1¼in) dice**
- **1 handful of coarsely chopped fresh flat-leaf parsley**

Pestos lend themselves to the inclusion of all manner of nuts and seeds, here it is pistachios, the herbs too are open to change, the requisite being they are soft and leafy and not overly pungent. Sorrel, a leaf that grows abundantly in my garden and on the surrounding hedgerow banks, makes a lovely and spontaneous pesto.

1. For the pilaf, preheat the oven to 200°C (fan 180°C/gas mark 6). Heat 2 tablespoons of olive oil in a large flameproof casserole dish over a medium heat and fry the shallots and peppers for about 5 minutes until softened, then stir in the coriander and cumin and fry for another 1–2 minutes until starting to colour, stirring frequently.

2. Stir in the spelt, pour in the stock, add the cinnamon stick, season and bring to the boil, then cover and cook in the oven for 15 minutes.

3. Scatter over the tomatoes and return to the oven for a further 20 minutes.

4. Five minutes before the end of this time, heat a large non-stick frying pan over a medium-high heat. Toss the chicken with the remaining tablespoon of olive oil in a medium bowl and season, then scatter over the base of the pan and sear to lightly colour, turning it with a spatula. Scatter this over the pilaf, then gently turn to mix the chicken and tomatoes into the spelt and cook for another 10 minutes or until the spelt is tender.

continued overleaf ▶

FOR THE PESTO

30g pistachios
40g fresh basil leaves
1 small garlic clove, peeled
4 tbsp extra virgin olive oil
squeeze of lemon juice

5. While the pilaf is cooking make the pesto. Gently toast the nuts in a medium frying pan over a medium-low heat for a few minutes until lightly coloured, shaking the pan now and again. Transfer to a food processor and leave to cool, then whizz to finely chop. Add the remaining ingredients for the pesto with a little salt and whizz to a purée.

6. Scatter the parsley over the pilaf and gently fold over to mix in, then repeat with the pesto.

TIPS FOR THE TABLE

The pilaf also makes a lovely side, for six, at any number of other occasions, in which case you can leave out the pesto and chicken. Add a couple of finely chopped garlic cloves with the spices.

VEGAN SWAP

For a vegan pilaf use vegetable stock and omit the chicken. Stir in a few warm cooked broad beans with the parsley at the end.

SERVES 2

READY IN 20 MINUTES

PESCATARIAN

SALMON AND SPINACH WITH RED LENTIL FUSILLI

- **20g fresh coriander (fine stalks and leaves)**
- **3 tbsp extra virgin olive oil**
- **1 tbsp lemon juice, plus a squeeze**
- **sea salt**
- **120g red lentil fusilli**
- **1 tsp finely chopped medium-hot red chilli**
- **1 garlic clove, peeled and finely chopped**
- **250g spinach**
- **125g skinless salmon fillet, cut into 2–3cm (¾–1¼in) dice**

Red lentil pasta has taken us by storm, even the large brands are onto it now, which is great news because you can hope to find it with some ease in a good-sized supermarket. This lively plate of pasta is as nutritious as it is zesty and vibrant, salmon, spinach and red lentils tizzed up with chilli, garlic and lemon. The perfect pasta supper for two.

1. Whizz the coriander with 2 tablespoons of oil, a squeeze of lemon juice and a little salt, to a purée in a food processor, scraping down the bowl as necessary, and scoop into a small bowl.

2. Bring a large pan of salted water to the boil, add the pasta, give it a stir and cook according to the packet instructions or until just tender, then drain into a colander and shake dry.

3. Meanwhile heat 1 tablespoon of oil in a large non-stick frying pan over a medium-high heat, stir the chilli and garlic into the oil, then add the spinach half at a time and fry until it wilts.

4. Stir in the salmon, cover with a lid and cook over a low heat for 3 minutes.

5. Scatter over a little salt, drizzle over a tablespoon of lemon juice and gently stir. Mix in the pasta and serve dotted with the herb purée.

SERVES 4

READY IN 30 MINUTES

VEGETARIAN

COURGETTE AND GOAT'S CHEESE WITH CHICKPEA PENNE

- **3 tbsp extra virgin olive oil, plus extra to serve**
- **700g courgettes, trimmed and sliced**
- **1 bunch of spring onions, trimmed and sliced**
- **4 garlic cloves, peeled and thinly sliced**
- **sea salt and freshly ground black pepper**
- **100ml vegetarian white wine**
- **1 handful of fresh mint, plus a few tiny leaves**
- **300g chickpea penne**
- **100g soft goat's cheese, coarsely crumbled**
- **grated vegetarian Parmesan-style cheese to serve**

This recipe shows how a classic pasta dish can be reformulated for maximum nutrition. The breakdown of ingredients amounts to legumes (chickpeas), vegetables (courgettes, spring onions, garlic), healthy fat (extra virgin olive oil) and a helping of dairy.

1. Heat the olive oil in a large saucepan over a medium-low heat, add the courgettes, spring onion and garlic, season and fry for 15–20 minutes until soft and translucent, stirring frequently.

2. Add the wine, turn the heat up and simmer until well-reduced.

3. Liquidise the contents of the pan in a blender with the mint, then taste for seasoning. Return the sauce to the pan.

4. Meanwhile bring a large pan of salted water to the boil, add the pasta, give it a stir and cook according to the packet instructions or until just tender. Drain it into a colander, reheat the sauce and mix in the pasta, and gently fold in the goat's cheese.

5. Serve scattered with cheese, a drizzle of oil and a few tiny mint leaves.

SERVES 2

READY IN 25 MINUTES

FLEXITARIAN

ROAST CHICKEN AND MUSHROOMS WITH SPELT CASARECCE

- sea salt and freshly ground black pepper
- 150g spelt casarecce
- 2 tbsp extra virgin olive oil, plus extra to serve
- 2 shallots, peeled and finely chopped
- 400g chestnut mushrooms, trimmed and sliced
- 100ml white wine
- 30g finely grated Parmesan
- 150g cooked free-range roast chicken, thinly sliced

If you do have a hankering for roast chicken one Sunday, this is a good way of spreading the meat over a number of meals in the days that follow. A deliciously creamy mushroom sauce with slivers of chicken, super-comforting and a good one for a weekday. Spelt pasta, like red lentil pasta, has been popularized, and as such comes in all manner of shapes.

1. You can either make the sauce in advance of cooking the pasta, or at the same time. Bring a large pan of salted water to the boil, add the pasta, give it a stir and cook according to the packet instructions or until just tender.

2. Heat a large non-stick frying pan over a medium-high heat, add 1 tablespoon of olive oil, then half the shallots and cook briefly until translucent. Throw in half the mushrooms, and fry for about 3 minutes, stirring occasionally until golden. Don't worry about any liquid given out, this will add to the sauce. Remove and cook the remainder in the same way. Return all the shallots and mushrooms to the pan, add the wine and simmer to reduce by about half.

3. Transfer half the mushrooms and any liquid to a blender, add 100ml water, two thirds of the Parmesan and some seasoning and purée until smooth and silky, adding a little more water if necessary. Stir this back in with the rest of the mushrooms.

continued overleaf ▶

4. Add the chicken and heat through.

5. Drain the pasta into a colander and stir into the sauce. Serve scattered with the rest of the Parmesan and an extra drizzle of oil.

TIP

For a creamier mushroom sauce add a little crème fraîche or soured cream to the finished sauce.

SERVES 4
READY IN 15–20 MINUTES
PESCATARIAN

NO-COOK CRAB AND BUCKWHEAT SPAGHETTI

FOR THE SAUCE

200g mixture brown and white crabmeat
1 medium-hot red chilli, core and seeds discarded, and finely chopped
1 garlic clove, peeled and crushed to a paste
6 tbsp extra virgin olive oil
4 tbsp lemon juice
2 heaped tbsp coarsely chopped fresh flat-leaf parsley, plus extra to serve
sea salt and freshly ground black pepper

FOR THE PASTA

300g buckwheat spaghetti

This no-cook crab pasta has been doing its lap of honour ever since the River Café made it a part of their repertoire. Relying on a generous dose of olive oil, with no additional high-fat cheese, it has always struck a healthy note, and here this is taken one step further by replacing the usual refined white pasta with buckwheat pasta. Spelt pasta is another option.

1. Combine all the ingredients for the sauce in a large bowl.

2. Bring a large pan of water to the boil and cook the pasta according to the instructions, drain into a colander and toss with the sauce.

3. Serve scattered with a little more parsley.

SERVES 4

READY IN 1 HOUR 10 MINUTES–1 HOUR 15 MINUTES

FLEXITARIAN

BLACK BEAN SPAGHETTI WITH SAUSAGE AND PEPPERS

600g tomatoes, halved
3 tbsp extra virgin olive oil
sea salt and freshly ground black pepper
6 long red peppers, core and seeds removed and thickly sliced
4 pork sausages, such as chorizo-style, Toulouse, or Lincolnshire
2 red onions, peeled, halved and thinly sliced
2 tsp balsamic vinegar
130g black bean spaghetti – I like Liberto
coarsely chopped fresh flat-leaf parsley to serve

Sausage and beans but not as we know it. Black bean spaghetti is lovely stuff, high in protein so you only need a fraction of a normal pasta, guaranteed to leave you feeling well-fed for hours afterwards. This is my take on a super simple meatball-style of pasta.

1. Preheat the oven to 210°C (fan 190°C/gas mark 6). Arrange the tomatoes, cut-side up, in a single layer in a roasting tin, drizzle over 1 tablespoon of oil and season. Spread the peppers over the base of another large roasting tin, drizzle over 2 tablespoons of oil, season and toss to coat. If the sausages have skins, slit and slip these off, then break the sausagemeat into 2–3cm (¾–1¼in) pieces and scatter on top of the peppers. Roast both tins for 30 minutes, then stir the onions into the peppers.

2. Roast for another 15 minutes, then remove the tomatoes. Stir the peppers and sausages and cook these for a further 15 minutes. At the same time put a pan of salted water on to boil for the pasta.

3. Whizz the tomatoes with the balsamic vinegar and a little salt to a purée in a blender, as thoroughly as possible.

4. Add the pasta to the boiling water just before the peppers and sausages are done; stir and simmer according to the packet instructions or until just tender. Drain it into a colander, shake dry and return it to the pan. Add the tomato sauce and gently toss; if necessary, briefly reheat.

5. Pile the spaghetti onto four plates, spoon the peppers and sausage on top and scatter with parsley.

SERVES 4

READY IN 25–30 MINUTES

VEGETARIAN

WATERCRESS AND ASPARAGUS WITH GREEN PEA PENNE

- **300g trimmed asparagus**
- **4 tbsp extra virgin olive oil, plus extra to serve**
- **3 garlic cloves, peeled and halved lengthways**
- **200g watercress**
- **1 large handful of coarsely chopped fresh flat-leaf parsley**
- **1 tbsp lemon juice**
- **sea salt and freshly ground black pepper**
- **250g green pea penne**
- **grated vegetarian Parmesan-style cheese to serve**

We can't find too many ways of enjoying green peas and asparagus together, such as this take on the classic marriage. Like the Chickpea penne on page 206, it is light and healthy, and green.

1. For the sauce, cut off and reserve the asparagus tips and thickly slice the remaining stalks.

2. Drizzle 1 tablespoon of oil over the base of a large saucepan, scatter over the garlic and sliced asparagus, pile the watercress on top and add 150ml water. Now cover with a lid and cook over a gentle heat for 15 minutes until the asparagus is tender and the leaves have wilted, stirring towards the end.

3. Meanwhile bring a medium pan of water to the boil and blanch the asparagus tips for 2 minutes, then drain into a sieve.

4. Whizz the contents of the watercress pan with the parsley, remaining oil, lemon juice and some seasoning to a smooth purée in a blender. Return this to the pan.

5. Meanwhile bring a large pan of salted water to the boil, add the pasta, give it a stir and cook according to the packet instructions or until just tender.

6. Drain the pasta into a colander, reheat the sauce, add the pasta and toss to coat it. Spread the pasta over the base of four shallow bowls, scatter over the asparagus tips, then liberally dust with cheese, and drizzle over a little more oil.

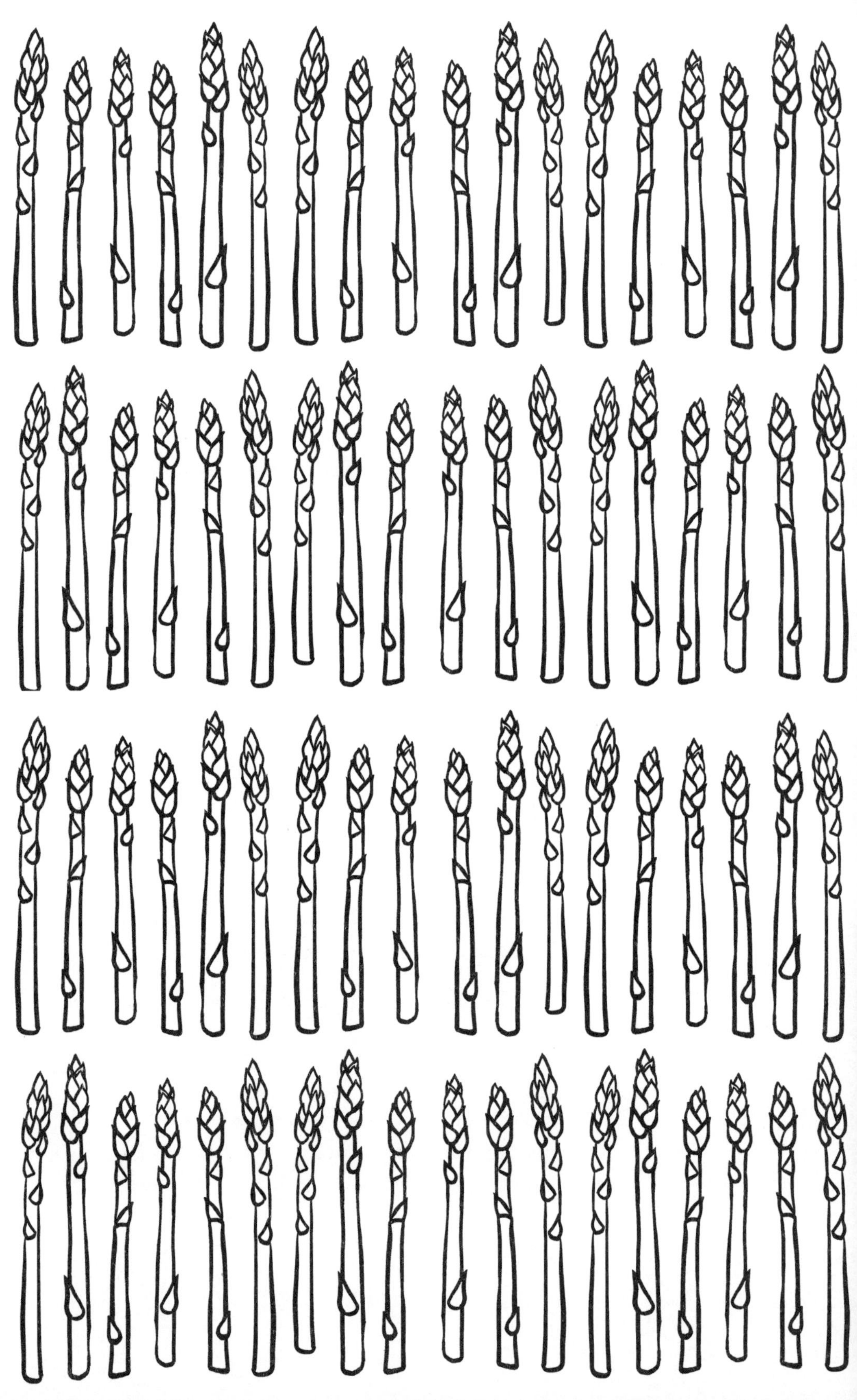

PLANETARY HEALTH DIET CHALLENGE

The key with this diet is to adopt a pattern of eating through your choice of foods, and for most of us it is likely this will involve change. So, to get into the habit, why not treat the meal plan below as a challenge and try to follow it over the course of a week. It will soon become second nature.

The second part of the challenge lies with reducing food waste. The chapter Waste not, want not (see page 24) sets out the potential pitfalls that lead to us throwing food away, with suggestions on how to save more. The aim is to halve our food waste. So at the same time as following the meal plan, why not keep a rough diary of what you are throwing out, and look for ways of reducing this. There is nothing like putting something in writing to bring it into focus.

MEAL PLAN

This meal plan serves as a handy tool to show how the Planetary Health Diet might work in practice. The Monday through to Sunday diary takes in breakfast through to supper, with suggestions for snacks in between. But as we all have different appetites, and the last thing I want is to give you yet another set of rules that has you religiously weighing everything out, simply tailor these suggestions to your own lifestyle.

It may be that you are a three-square-meals-a-day person, avoiding snacks, or that, like me, you are bird-like of appetite and thrive off a stream of light bites that amounts to grazing from dawn to dusk. And we all have differing energy needs depending on our age, how active we are and our size. The Planetary Health Diet is based on an intake of 2,500 kcal per day, the average energy needs for a man weighing 70kg aged 30 years or a woman weighing 60kg aged 30 years, with a moderate to high level of physical activity. But, assuming you are maintaining a healthy weight, there is no need to change the amounts you are eating. After a week, if you do happen to think you are gaining weight, then simply reduce portion size.

You also need to factor in what you drink. As a nutritionist, if I am advising about losing weight, my first thought goes to 'what are you drinking?' (and I don't mean wine). It's the milky coffees, the smoothies and the sweetened drinks, frequently dressed up as health drinks, that are the culprits. For most of us, cutting out the energy derived from drinks is the simplest way of reducing our calorie intake, without going hungry. My son says one of the things he thanks me for as a teenager was my insistence that he didn't take sugar in his tea. So I would suggest aiming to drink 'unsweetened' tea and coffee, with a little skimmed milk if wished, and water, throughout the day. I'm not a great fan of fruit juices either; there is always more to be gained, both in pleasure and nutrition, from eating the whole fruit. I find real food far too enjoyable to sacrifice calories to a sweetened drink.

The overall dietary pattern is to eat a plant-based diet from breakfast through to supper, including a portion of dairy if wished (see page 16). So this should include breakfast, lunch, tea and any snacks. The ideal is to draw from all four plant-based food groups: vegetables and fruits, legumes, whole grains and nuts. This can be tailored for vegans by omitting dairy produce. Supper is where different dietary preferences come into play, depending on whether you are vegan, vegetarian, pescatarian or flexitarian (see page 18).

As you will be eating whole natural foods throughout the day, including when you are snacking, to ease the potential workload, supper is the only time when you need to don an apron and actually cook. Although when I am working at home, I like to spread cooking throughout the day: a little tinkering in the kitchen is a good way of taking a break. Whenever possible though, try to think ahead to the next day's lunch or day after by cooking extra, especially of veggies and grains. Combining this approach with shopping for healthy basics that require no or minimal prep, it should be easy enough to adopt this way of eating without excessive work.

BREAKFAST

Breakfast is the ideal time to work some whole grains into our day, and they make for pretty perfect sustenance by slowly releasing energy throughout the morning at a time when we need it the most. There is little to beat a bowl of porridge (see page 230), which can be dressed in any number of ways. Mixed-grain porridges are also an excellent way of deriving a broad range of nutrients. Granola too offers up a spectrum of goodness from whole grains, nuts and dried fruits (see page 229). A thick slab of wholegrain toast is another route, especially if it is spread with avocado, or served with grilled tomatoes or fried mushrooms, with Nut butter dressing (see page 235) or nut butter, working in some vegetables and nuts and avoiding the trap of butter and jam.

The meal plan suggests all of these, but that is not to say that you need to have a different breakfast every day of the week. Most of us are creatures of habit when it comes to breakfast, half asleep and on auto-pilot. When trying to get yourself to work or your children to school, the last thing you want is a 7 a.m. challenge. So vary it as suits. I find there will be one or two mornings a week when I am porridge-hungry and in need of a big bowl of warming carby nourishment, while on other mornings I might prefer something lighter, like berries with a little yoghurt and some granola.

LUNCH

A decent mid-week lunch has everything to do with planning in advance, ensuring that you have plenty of raw materials to hand to throw together a speedy nutritious bite. Mezze shows us the way here: basically any line-up of bits and pieces that amounts to grazing.

I would also throw in making a big pot of soup every now and again and freezing it in batches (see page 40).

SUPPER

Supper is the time to enjoy a little chicken or fish, an egg dish or the weekly treat of some beef, pork or lamb. The recipe chapters lead you through how to make the most of these foods, in a way that also fits with other recommendations in the Planetary Health Diet. Here, the key to making your life easy is to think ahead, and always cook extra of any ingredient that you can see might have a second life as the material for lunch (see Extra supper ingredients, page 218).

The flexitarian weekly meal plan allows for poultry on two days a week, fish on two days a week (I would recommend oily fish at least once), meat and eggs on one day each, with a vegetarian supper on the seventh day. This is the maximum in relation to animal protein, but you can also exchange chicken and poultry for eggs, fish or plant protein. Legumes, peanuts, tree nuts, seeds and soy protein are also interchangeable. Over to you.

SNACKS

Like breakfast and lunch, snacks should focus on plant foods. This is a particularly good time to sneak in a few extra veg by way of crudités and leftover cooked veggies, and as dips and soups too. I would suggest eating a little fruit at breakfast, and then one other piece during the day, and I always try to ensure one of these amounts to a bowl of berries, which are low in carbs.

- Banana cake or muffins
- Crudités, simply boiled veg and roast veg with dip, e.g. Nut butter dressing (see page 235), guacamole, tzatziki, roast vegetable dip or hummus
- Wholegrain crackers, bread sticks or pittas with dip (as above)

- Cheese oatcakes (see page 233)
- Granola – by the handful
- Berries
- Citrus, exotic and orchard fruits
- Natural or Greek yoghurt – with fruit, with a few cooked whole grains stirred through or a drizzle of date or maple syrup
- Nuts – peanuts, walnuts, pistachios, pecans, brazil nuts or cashews
- Seeds – sunflower seeds, pine nuts or pumpkin seeds (see page 45)
- Riches from the rubble soup (see page 40)
- Lentil crisps
- Plain or salted popcorn
- Dates with goat's cheese

EXTRA SUPPER INGREDIENTS

I always cook more of any ingredient or component of supper that will be good cold a day or two after.

Simple boiled or steamed veg

Broccoli spears, green beans, sugar snaps, mangetouts, asparagus, peas, broad beans, soya (edamame beans), cauliflower, chard

Simple roast veg

Peppers, courgettes, aubergine, beetroot, carrots, asparagus, broccoli, cauliflower, sweet potato, butternut squash, leeks

Dips and dressings

Pesto*, herb purées, chickpea and pulse dips, salad dressings, Nut butter dressing**

Simple boiled whole grains

Spelt, freekeh, brown, red or black rice, wild rice, wheat berries, quinoa, buckwheat (see individual recipes)

STORECUPBOARD CONVENIENCE

Whole grains and pulses
Sachets of cooked brown rice, quinoa, lentil and grain mixes, tinned pulses

Nuts
Unsalted and roasted nuts

Jars
Tahini, nut butters

Pickles
Pickled chillies, beetroot, artichokes, walnuts, semi-dried tomatoes, olives

Seaweed
Dried seaweed

FRIDGE MATERIAL

See also Extra supper ingredients (left)

Veggie protein
Tofu – firm, silken or smoked

Dairy
Natural and Greek yoghurt, young goat's and curd cheeses, mozzarella, feta, Emmental, Gruyère, halloumi

Salad drawer
Tomatoes, salad leaves, salad sprouts, avocados, spring onions

Riches from the rubble soup
See page 40

MEAL PLAN KEY

Recipes marked with * can be found in the recipe chapters; those with ** are supporting bonus recipes in this chapter (see page 228); those with (**V** option) are the vegetarian options for recipes in the recipe chapters; and those with (**L**) make use of leftovers from your cooking on a previous day in the plan.

MEAL PLAN WEEK 1

Flexitarian with vegetarian options

	BREAKFAST	LUNCH
MONDAY	Wholegrain toast with Avo nut butter** and sprouting seeds	Fiery chickpea dip* with crudités Wholegrain bruschettas with Roast tomatoes* Simple rocket salad with crumbled goat's cheese
TUESDAY	Figgy granola** with milk	Quinoa and sugar snaps (**L**) tossed with steamed green beans, with Nut butter dressing** Papaya and lime
WEDNESDAY	Wholegrain toast with almond butter and grilled tomatoes	Miso-glazed courgette and peppers* (**L**) with edamame beans (**L**) and buckwheat Pomegranate seeds and blackberries with Greek yoghurt
THURSDAY	Berry banana smoothie* Sticky granola balls**	Salad of freekeh (**L**) tossed with roast vegetables (**L**) and olives
FRIDAY	Bircher muesli** (with added spelt grains)	Salad of broad beans, and roast peppers (**L**), tossed with rocket, cherry tomatoes and pine nuts Peach compote and coconut yoghurt
SATURDAY	Greek yoghurt with Figgy granola** and blueberries	Spinach and scamorza pizza omelette* Courgette chips* Wholemeal bruschettas with Roast tomatoes (**L**)*
SUNDAY	Multi-grain porridge** (e.g. amaranth porridge with wholegrain spelt added) with Greek yoghurt, cinnamon, raisins and pistachios Pear	Buckwheat pasta with Roast tomatoes* Steamed green beans and asparagus (**L**) with vinaigrette

Try to get ahead with some cooking on Sunday: the dip and tomatoes for Monday can be made in advance, as can granola for breakfasts.

SUPPER	TIPS
Quinoa and sugar snap stir-fry* Baby spinach salad	*Make extra dip and freeze for Sunday supper* *Cook extra roast tomatoes for Saturday lunch* *Cook extra stir-fry for Tuesday lunch*
Thai chicken and edamame bean curry* Miso-glazed courgette and peppers* Lemon and pine nut brown rice pilaf*	*Cook extra miso-glazed vegetables and edamame beans for Wednesday lunch*
Crispy salmon with freekeh and cavolo* or Tomato spelt with basil and pistachio pesto* (**V** option) Roast aubergine and red peppers	*Cook extra freekeh for Thursday lunch and roast vegetables for Thursday and Friday lunches*
Spinach and millet porridge with cashews* Simple green salad with avocado	
Seabass fish fingers with tartare sauce* with Pea and mint mash* or Spicy cauli with turmeric yoghurt* with green lentils (**V** option) Steamed green beans and asparagus	*Cook extra green beans and asparagus for Sunday lunch, and extra cauliflower if having vegetarian option for Saturday supper*
Lamb, date and tomato tagine* or Coconut dal curry* (**V** option) Spicy cauli (**L**) with turmeric yoghurt* Bulgur wheat pilaf*	
Crispy chicken thighs with fiery chickpea dip* (**L**), or replace chicken thighs with Roast Romanesco and spring onion salad with balsamic vinegar* (**V** option) Bulgur wheat, cashew nut and rocket pilaf*	

MEAL PLAN WEEK 2

Flexitarian

	BREAKFAST	LUNCH
MONDAY	As for Week 1	Red pepper confit* and Lentil pasta salad Grapes and apple
TUESDAY	As for Week 1	Buckwheat (**L**), pecan, rocket, avocado, and pomegranate (**L**) salad Figs, Greek yoghurt and date syrup
WEDNESDAY	As for Week 1	Salad of white beans (**L**) with chopped radish, cucumber, celery and parsley Papaya and lime Sticky granola balls*
THURSDAY	As for Week 1	Salad of spelt, with roast vegetables (**L**) and olives
FRIDAY	As for Week 1	Riches from the rubble soup* Banana and pineapple
SATURDAY	As for Week 1	Red pepper confit* and Wholemeal bruschettas with tomatoes Melon and passionfruit
SUNDAY	As for Week 1 but with coconut yoghurt replacing Greek yoghurt	Peas, French beans and sugar snaps (**L**) with chopped walnuts and fiery chickpea dip* or hummus Wholemeal wraps Strawberries, blackberries and blueberries

SUPPER	TIPS
Chicken and broad bean stew with pomegranate* Buckwheat with olive oil and parsley	*Prepare extra pomegranate and buckwheat for Tuesday lunch*
Garlicky white beans with spinach* Mixed tomato salad (see Tip, page 173)	*Cook extra white beans for Wednesday lunch*
Roast chicken with roots and persillade* Broccoli mash with sesame seeds*	*Roast an extra tray of veg for Thursday lunch*
Simply salmon and pea fish stew* Wholegrain croutons Griddled asparagus with Nut butter dressing**	
Healthy Planet burgers* Celeriac wedges*	*Make extra soup and freeze for Week 3 Monday Lunch*
Fish pie with pecan crumble* Peas, French beans and sugar snaps	*Cook extra veg for Sunday lunch*
Ranchos eggs with cauliflower and lentils* Straw celeriac cake* Green salad with avocado	

MEAL PLAN WEEK 3

Flexitarian

	BREAKFAST	LUNCH
MONDAY	As for Week 1	Riches from the rubble soup* (**L**) with lentils Plum compote, Greek yoghurt and blackberries
TUESDAY	As for Week 1	Quinoa (**L**) and roast aubergine salad, with Nut butter dressing** Peaches and fresh goat's cheese
WEDNESDAY	As for Week 1	Roast cabbage (**L**) with spelt, chopped date and coriander salad Pear with blue cheese
THURSDAY	As for Week 1	Salad of orange and beetroot (**L**), chard (**L**) and lentils
FRIDAY	As for Week 1	Salad of beetroot, asparagus and freekeh (**L**) Pomegranate seeds and coconut yoghurt
SATURDAY	As for Week 1	Wholemeal bruschettas, with broad bean guacamole (**L**), roast peppers and pickled chillies Medley of melons
SUNDAY	As for Week 1 but with coconut yoghurt replacing Greek yoghurt	Salad of root veg (**L**) with quinoa, lamb's lettuce and pine nuts Mango and pineapple

SUPPER	TIPS
Chilli prawn and chickpea stew* Quinoa with olive oil and chopped coriander Simple baby spinach salad	*Cook extra quinoa for Tuesday lunch*
Chicken and mushroom pie with cauliflower mash* Roast cabbage with almonds*	*Cook extra cabbage for Wednesday lunch*
Sesame mackerel with orange and beetroot salad* Wilted chard with garlic Steamed potato and pea salad with mayonnaise	*Make extra Orange and beetroot salad, and cook extra wilted chard for Thursday lunch*
Paprika chicken with pecan and coriander salsa* Roast beetroot and asparagus roast* (with added freekeh or wild rice)	*Make extra beetroot, asparagus and freekeh for Friday lunch*
Corn tortillas with broad bean guacamole and fried eggs* Beetroot mash with wild mushrooms* and fried halloumi slices (optional)	*Make extra guacamole for Saturday lunch*
Healthy Planet chilli con carne* Lemon and pine nut brown rice pilaf* Honey and sesame roast roots* Green salad	*Make extra roast veg for Sunday lunch*
Speedy cauliflower, lentil and watercress risotto* Simple rocket, blue cheese and walnut salad	

MEAL PLAN WEEK 4

Flexitarian

	BREAKFAST	LUNCH
MONDAY	As for Week 1	Wholemeal pittas with beetroot, hummus and goat's cheese Strawberries and banana
TUESDAY	As for Week 1	Silken tofu with sesame** Salad of watercress, rocket and baby spinach Papaya and lime
WEDNESDAY	As for Week 1	Miso-glazed courgette and peppers* (**L**) with buckwheat Pomegranate seeds and blackberries with Greek yoghurt
THURSDAY	As for Week 1	Salad of freekeh with padrón peppers (**L**), chopped cherry tomatoes and olives Kiwi fruit and lime
FRIDAY	As for Week 1	Green vegetable minestrone (**L**) with mint and almond pesto* Wholemeal rolls Figs and passionfruit
SATURDAY	As for Week 1	Spinach and scamorza pizza omelette* Courgette chips* Wholemeal bruschettas
SUNDAY	As for Week 1	Spinach, nut and goat's cheese pie* (**L**) Tomato salad (see Tip, page 173) Cherries, raspberries and blueberries

SUPPER	TIPS
Green vegetable minestrone with mint and almond pesto* Wholemeal rolls	*Make extra soup and freeze for Friday lunch*
Scallop tikka* Miso-glazed courgette and peppers* Lemon and pine nut brown rice pilaf*	*Cook extra miso-glazed vegetables and soya (edamame) beans for Wednesday lunch*
Chicken with spinach and padrón peppers* Haricot bean smash*	*Cook extra peppers for Thursday lunch*
Salmon salad Niçoise* Chargrilled broccoli or asparagus	
Seared tuna with cucumber and edamame salsa* Buttered udon noodles	
Spinach, nut and goat's cheese pie* Simple green salad with broad beans	*Leftover pie for Sunday lunch*
Healthy Planet steak and mash* Green beans and asparagus	

MEAL PLAN: BONUS RECIPES

AVO NUT BUTTER

SERVES 2

READY IN 10 MINUTES

VEGAN

1 avocado, halved, pitted and peeled
1 tbsp lemon juice
30g smooth or crunchy peanut butter
sea salt, to taste

Spread onto toast, this is a neat way of getting whole grains, nuts and a vegetable into breakfast. It is ultimately adaptable, any nut butter will serve; in addition to the many on offer you can make your own (see page 235). Pistachio and pecan butters are a personal favourite.

1. Whizz all the ingredients together in a food processor until smooth.

FIGGY GRANOLA

SERVES 10 (MAKES APPROXIMATELY 600G)

READY IN 1 HOUR

VEGETARIAN

FOR THE SYRUP

150g honey
2 tbsp vegetable oil
1 heaped tsp ground cinnamon
1 tsp vanilla bean paste

FOR THE GRANOLA MIX

250g whole rolled or jumbo oats
90g hazelnuts, coarsely chopped
25g sesame seeds
25g desiccated coconut (optional)
100g dried figs

This is a really easy basic. Here I've used honey to sweeten it but I often use maple or date syrup too. And the dried fruit and nuts are also open to interpretation. Unlike many commercial granolas, which have all sorts of additives, this recipe is 'true' to its ingredients and is not as sweet.

1. Preheat the oven to 150°C (fan 130°C/gas mark 2). Gently heat all the syrup ingredients together in a medium non-stick saucepan, stirring occasionally, until thin and amalgamated.

2. Add the oats, nuts and sesame seeds and stir to coat. Spread the mixture in a thin layer over the base of a large roasting tin (e.g. 25 x 38cm/10 x 15in). Roast for 45 minutes until lightly toasted, stirring every 15 minutes, and stirring in the coconut, if wished, after 30 minutes.

3. Chop the figs into pieces the size of raisins and mix into the granola, separating out the pieces, and leave to cool before storing in a sealed container.

SERVES 2

READY IN 10 MINUTES

VEGAN

WHOLE OAT PORRIDGE

100g whole rolled porridge oats
sea salt (optional)

A foundation porridge at its simplest.

1. Combine the oats with 600ml water in a small non-stick saucepan, bring to the boil and simmer, stirring, over a low heat for 6–7 minutes until thick and creamy.

2. Add a pinch of salt at the end if wished. Serve as suggested opposite.

VARIATION

VEGAN

MULTI-GRAIN PORRIDGE

There are some excellent mixes on the market that are specially designed to cook together. If you want to make your own:

1. Make a foundation porridge using a grain that will turn nice and creamy – oats, amaranth, teff and millet are all ideal.

2. Stir 2–3 heaped tablespoons of cooked whole grains into the finished porridge to enrich the range of nutrients and give it additional bite – spelt, quinoa, brown rice, freekeh, buckwheat, wheat berries. This is where the bowl of grains in the fridge comes in so handy (see page 50).

3. Serve as suggested opposite.

SERVING IDEAS FOR PORRIDGE

Sweeten with a drizzle of date syrup, maple syrup or honey

Alternatively, sweeten with a stevia-based sweetener. Look for erythritol in the ingredients list, which offers the most natural flavour

Serve the porridge with a splash of milk or buttermilk, or a spoonful of yoghurt

Scatter with raspberries, blueberries, blackberries, sliced strawberries, sliced mango or papaya

Serve with a spoonful of homemade apple, pear, plum or peach compote

Scatter with toasted chopped hazelnuts, toasted almonds, sliced pecans or walnut pieces

Stir a tablespoon of flaxseed meal into the finished porridge for added fibre and omega-3 oils

SERVES 4

READY IN 15 MINUTES PLUS OVERNIGHT SOAKING

VEGETARIAN

BIRCHER MUESLI

120g rolled oats
250g full or low-fat Greek yoghurt
½ tsp vanilla extract
75g raspberries
75g red or green seedless grapes, halved
6 tsp maple syrup
20g pistachios, finely chopped

The tradition of a proper overnight Bircher muesli has stayed with me since the age of five, when a Swiss au-pair introduced it to our household. So I regard a big mixing bowl of oats soaking in water on the counter come bedtime as promise of a treat early morning. As with porridge, any soft fruit can be included here, likewise nuts and syrup. Vegans can use a soya yoghurt in lieu of Greek – I like to make my own by whizzing a soft tofu in a food processor until it is smooth and creamy, which is also good for adding in plant protein.

1. Place the oats in a large bowl, cover plentifully with cold water and set aside in a cool place or the fridge to soak overnight.

2. Drain the oats into a sieve, give it a couple of shakes and return them to a large bowl. Stir in the yoghurt and the vanilla, then mix in two thirds of the raspberries and grapes. Spoon the porridge into four bowls, drizzle a teaspoon of syrup over each one and turn a couple of times to marble it, then drizzle over another half-teaspoon and scatter with the remaining fruit and nuts.

MAKES 15–20 OATCAKES
READY IN 45–50 MINUTES
VEGETARIAN

CHEESE OATCAKES

90g whole rolled oats
60g wholemeal spelt flour
¼ tsp bicarbonate of soda
¼ tsp fine sea salt
60g finely grated vegetarian Parmesan-style cheese
2 tbsp rapeseed oil
boiling water

Super easy, there's no resting the dough and no messy floured work surface either. They're a great basic from breakfast time onwards: a few snatched as a snack on the way to work, or for dipping and spreading.

1. Preheat the oven to 160°C (140°C fan/gas mark 3). Whizz the oats, flour, bicarb, salt and two thirds of the cheese to a fine meal in a food processor. Add the oil and whizz again, then add just enough boiling water (about 3 tbsp) to bring the dough together.

2. Lay out a large sheet of baking parchment or greaseproof paper on the work surface, place the dough in the centre, and lay another sheet on top. Pat the dough to flatten it, then with a rolling pin, roll it out to a thickness of approximately 3mm (⅛ in).

3. Peel off the top sheet of baking parchment or greaseproof paper, cut the dough into 6–8cm (2½–3¼in) squares and halve these into triangles. Carefully lift onto a non-stick baking sheet using a spatula or palette knife, and scatter over the remaining cheese. Bake for 30–35 minutes, until the oatcakes are crisp and the cheese is golden. Leave to cool on the baking sheet before storing in an airtight container. They will keep well for at least a week.

STICKY GRANOLA BALLS

MAKES 20 BALLS

READY IN 20 MINUTES PLUS CHILLING

VEGAN

100g sunflower seeds
50g stoned Medjool dates
1 tsp finely grated orange zest
30g coconut oil
100g granola
25ml orange juice
50g poppy seeds (optional)

A healthy melange of seeds, dates and granola, these soft fudgey balls make for an indulgent snack breakfast, full of energy and nutrients, and you can eat them on the go. They also lend themselves to lunchboxes.

1. Whizz the sunflower seeds in a food processor for several minutes to form a very fine meal.

2. Add the dates and orange zest and continue to process until finely chopped, then add the coconut oil and whizz to a sticky paste.

3. Add the granola, and continue to whizz to a fine crumble, then add the juice to achieve a firm sticky dough.

4. Roll heaped teaspoons of the mixture into balls slightly smaller than a walnut. They should each weigh about 15g. Either roll in the poppy seeds, in a small bowl to coat them, or leave them plain as preferred. Arrange on a plate spaced slightly apart, cover and chill for a couple of hours. These will keep well for a good week. They can be eaten chilled or at room temperature.

SERVES 4

READY IN 10 MINUTES

VEGAN

NUT BUTTER DRESSING

100g pecan nuts
sea salt
cayenne pepper, to taste
1 tbsp lemon juice

This all-rounder can be whizzed up using any nut butter. If you have a jar of peanut, almond or cashew in the cupboard then you're halfway there. I like to indulge my love of pecans and pistachios by making my own.

I am happy to slather this on a hearty slab of spelt toast with wilted spinach at breakfast, or again at lunch with tomatoes, avocado and salad sprouts, or I use it as a dip for crudités. It's also office friendly, if you take it in a little pot to have with a salad.

1. Whizz the nuts with a little salt and cayenne pepper in a food processor to chop them finely, then continue to whizz for about 3 minutes, scraping down the bowl as they stick to the sides, until you have a creamy nut butter.

2. Add the lemon juice and then about 4 tablespoons of water, one at a time, until the dressing is the consistency of salad cream. Transfer to a bowl, cover and chill until required.

SILKEN TOFU WITH SESAME

SERVES 2

READY IN 5 MINUTES

VEGAN

2 tsp dark soy sauce
2 tsp lemon juice
2 tsp toasted sesame oil
200g silken tofu, cut into 4 slices
1 tsp sesame seeds
2 tsp finely chopped spring onion

This quick and simple recipe can be enjoyed as an addition to lunch or supper, or alone as a tasty snack.

1. Combine the soy sauce, lemon juice and sesame oil in a small dipping bowl to make a sauce.

2. Very carefully, so as not to break them, lay the tofu slices out on two small plates. Scatter with the sesame seeds and the spring onion. Serve with the sauce drizzled over.

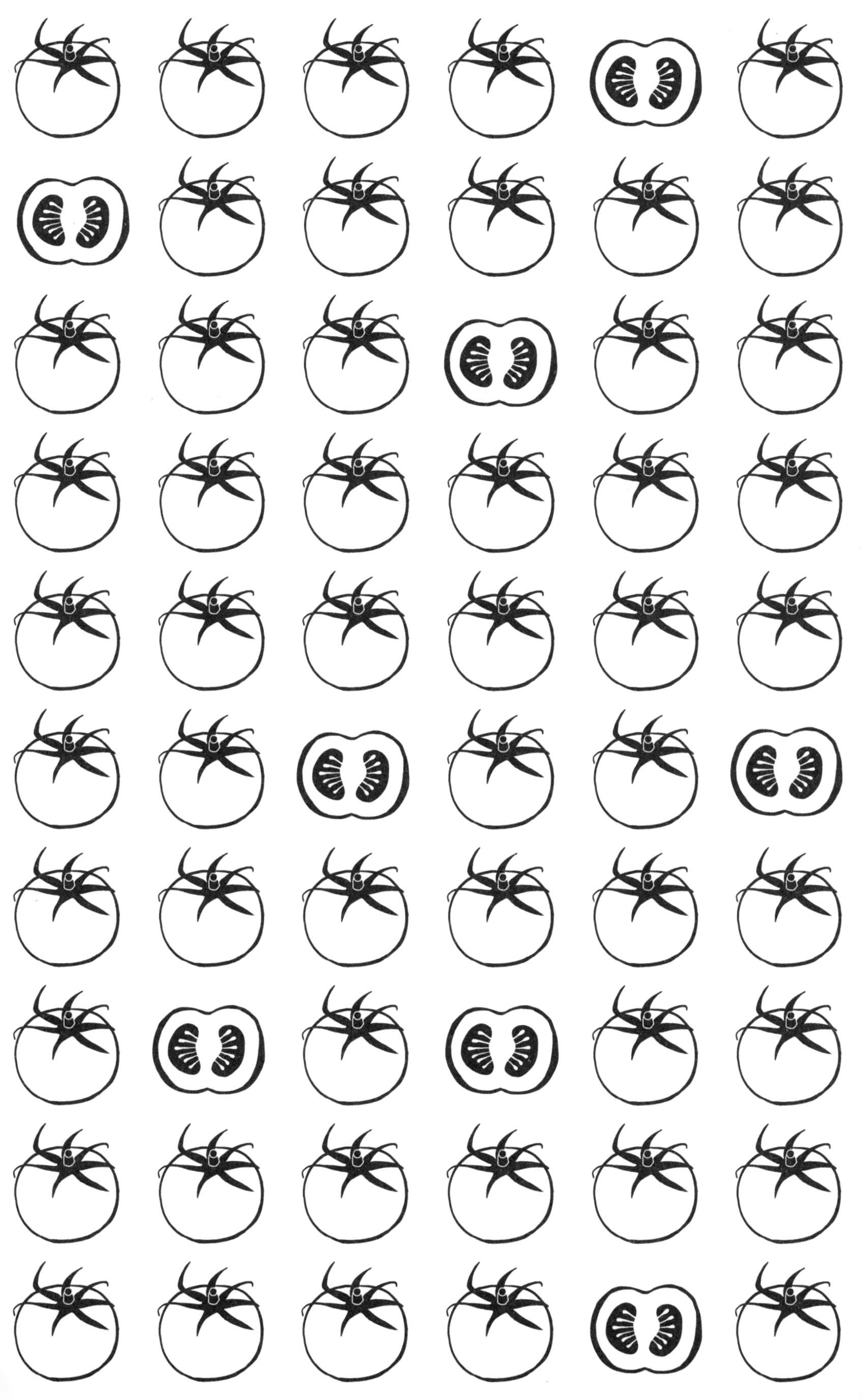

APPENDIX A: PLANETARY HEALTH DIET SCIENTIFIC TARGETS

Earth system 1 : Climate change

The issue
Climate change is uppermost in our awareness for its links to extreme weather and sea level rise, which are driven by the emission of the three greenhouse gases, carbon dioxide, methane and nitrous oxide.

Carbon dioxide
When land is tilled or burnt for agriculture, it creates CO_2 emissions, as do the fossil fuels that drive agricultural machinery and are involved in transport.

Methane
Methane, which has 56 times the warming potential of CO_2 over 20 years, is key to the controversy surrounding red meat, as it is produced by ruminant livestock such as cows and sheep during the digestion process. Less widely known are its links to rice production: it is given off by the decomposition of organic material in flooded rice paddies.

Nitrous oxide
Nitrous oxide has an incredible 280 times the warming potential of CO_2. This is emitted from soil microbes in croplands and pastures, and is in particular effected by fertilizer application.

The target

As there will always be some gas emissions from crop and livestock production, the goal is to reduce them and create a boundary. The Paris Agreement (see Notes, page 57) aims to restrict the global average temperature by 2100 to less than 2°C, but ideally closer to 1.5°C. To achieve this, a carbon budget consisting of all three gases has been proposed. So the world's food production systems will need to go from being a net carbon source to a net carbon sink,[1] and this will require the decarbonization of the energy system.

Earth system 2 : Freshwater use

The issue

Food production globally consumes more water than any other sector, and has more than doubled between 1961 and 2000. Water to land is what blood is to animals, and it drives nutrient cycles. Over 70 per cent of freshwater use is down to agriculture, but this feeds only 14 per cent of the total needed and very little of it can be reused. The remaining 86 per cent of water required is reliant on rain.

The target

Considering that plants transpire and water evaporates from the soil, there is only marginal manoeuvre for limiting freshwater water use in agriculture. Better irrigation technologies can play their part, but the main focus on saving will lie with industry and the domestic sectors who are better placed to take advantage of technological advances.

Water use could be improved through the trade of water-intensive food products between nations. Ironically, an impediment to this is our inclination to shop locally and for countries to be self-reliant, putting pressure on arid countries, where income is low and water consumption is high.

Earth systems 3 and 4 : Nitrogen and phosphorus flows

The issue

Both nitrogen and phosphorus are crucial for plant growth and for fertilizing croplands. Their availability will need to continue if we are to feed the world's population.

Nitrogen fertilizer is energy intensive and linked to high levels of reenhouse gas emissions, while phosphorus fertilizer is a non-renewable source mined from rock deposits, predicted to run out within 50–100 years. Freshwater and marine ecosystems are adversely affected by runoff into streams and rivers, which drives their eutrophication, causing fish to die. The excessive use of nitrogen in agriculture can also reduce biodiversity.

The target

To prevent nitrogen and phosphorus overuse, we need to close nutrient loops and use them efficiently, therefore also recycling nutrients in usable forms from places such as sewage treatment plants, compost operations and livestock production facilities.

There also needs to be a redistribution in the use of nitrogen: less in richer countries and more in developing countries that will benefit from greater yields.

Earth system 5 : Biodiversity loss (extinction rate)

The issue

Biodiversity, or the richness of living organisms in land and in water, contributes massively not only to food production, but also to pollination, pest control and the regulation of carbon sinks.

Agriculture is guilty of accounting for 80 per cent of extinction threats to mammal and bird species. And every species that is lost threatens our ability to respond to environmental change. In a study of protected areas, insect biomass has reduced by 75 per cent in 30 years and farmland birds by 30 per cent in 15 years.[2]

The target

Once biodiversity is lost the damage is done, and it can trigger irreversible changes, so the aim has to be for a lower extinction rate. The relevance of biodiversity in relation to food production starts with 'agrobiodiversity'.

This is a complex system that includes both cultivated and uncultivated foods – that we either eat or that support food production – but it also extends to soil microbiomes, insects, birds and mammals that pollinate crops, regulate pests and absorb excess nutrients.

Plants have brilliantly evolved many chemical means to protect themselves against predators and diseases, while their fruits and berries disperse seeds through animals.

It is so important for us to capitalize on their diversity through eating a wide range of fruits and vegetables, whole grains, legumes, seeds and nuts. But incredibly, we only eat some 150–200 plant species of an available 14,000 edible ones – rice, wheat and maize account for 60 per cent of calories consumed globally. So we need to make more of under-used edible plant species that can adapt to climate change and be more adventurous with our plant foods (see Grainology, page 47).

Earth system 6 : Cropland use (land-system change)

The issue

While the area of land mass used to produce food has remained almost constant since the middle of the last century, there has been a sinister shift in its allocation. Temperate regions such as Europe, Russia and North America occupy a smaller segment, while bio-diverse regions in the tropics such as Brazil, Indonesia and the Democratic Republic of Congo occupy a bigger segment.

When pressure to produce more food results in the clearing of dry and temperate forests and grasslands and, therefore, the burning of organisms within those areas, this in turn impacts on biodiversity loss and greenhouse-gas emissions.

The target

The aim is for a 'half earth' policy. If 50 per cent of the earth can be conserved as intact ecosystems, it is believed that we can thereby prevent further biodiversity loss and protect at least 80 per cent of pre-industrial species. But achieving this will necessitate halting the expansion of agriculture into forest areas and other natural ecosystems.

Hand in hand with this we need to revolutionize the intensification of agriculture by adopting sustainable practices for soil, water, nutrients and chemicals. Initiatives will include sustainable harvesting of native forests, and low-intensity grazing systems.

CONSUMER CHALLENGE

As consumers we can support the land-system by reducing our food loss and waste – the goal is by 50 per cent – and this will decrease the pressure on the demand for food. It is helpful to keep this link close to heart. When we save food, we are protecting ecosystems and biodiversity loss (see Waste not want not, page 24).

NOTES

1. A carbon sink absorbs more carbon than it releases, when it has the net effect of lowering atmospheric CO_2.
2. 'Food in the Anthropocene', p. 467.

APPENDIX B: BEFORE AND AFTER COVID-19

When I began writing this book, I could never in a million years have imagined the crisis that would engulf the world within months. And there have been times when the significance of climate change, the crusade of our times, has shrunk in magnitude.

And yet, to ignore or put it on the back burner would be a terrible and fatal mistake. While the pandemic and the environment might at a glance seem unrelated, they are intrinsically woven together. There's so much we don't know, but it seems almost certain that a trade in wildlife allowed a pathogen to jump the species barrier to humans, which was then transported around the world through modern travel. So, now more than ever, we should be using this calamitous event to redouble our efforts at saving the planet.

Much of what climate change activists have been campaigning for has been affected by this disaster. The first change was in our air. In cities, as the roads emptied of traffic and industrial estates stood idle, there was a noticeable change in the quality of the air, the haze cleared and the sky shone with a clarity normally only seen on an unspoilt area of the coast. We briefly tasted life beyond fossil fuels. As we stopped travelling to work domestically, and stopped flying to foreign destinations, our carbon footprints shrunk, and it felt as though the environment expanded, and wildlife ventured into new habitats.

The world will slowly return to pre-Covid-19 levels of activity. That return is a golden opportunity to try and steer our reliance on fossil fuels to greener sources of energy, and to harness the return at a political level in a positive way. We witnessed the power of the world coming together for a greater good. For the first time ever there was a common adversary and we fought it collectively, and if we can do it for a virus, we can do it for the health of the planet. The perceived 'naysayers' who feared and predicted a deadly global pandemic, and who were ignored, were on a parallel road to those seeking to highlight the dangers of climate change. There is a new optimism, a way of turning this tragic loss of life and livelihood into a driver for change.

HOW COVID-19 CHANGED US

Our approach to food waste is one area that has benefitted from this terrible situation. Public health departments couldn't have come up with a better strategy for overhauling our shopping habits. In a matter of days and weeks we totally reformed how we shopped, how we thought about food, what we valued, what we can live without, and what is most likely to go to waste, and therefore not worth buying. Whereas previously waste was unwanted, it became scarcely tolerated. Once you might have shopped on the off-chance that you would eat something, but didn't, and so it was thrown away. This became no longer acceptable in many people's eyes.

In essence, the pandemic injected a shot of much-needed sensitivity into the arena. We became much more aware. We thought before we bought. It remains to be seen if the trends and habits that we acquired during lockdown will continue into the long term. But certainly some of the value we now place on food waste is likely to colour our thinking for the foreseeable future.

ABOUT THE AUTHOR

Annie Bell (ANutr) is a Cookery Writer and Registered Associate Nutritionist with a Master's Degree in Human Nutrition.

She spent the early days of her career training as a chef, including at Kensington Place under Rowley Leigh. Her first food column was as *Vogue*'s cookery writer, before she joined the *Independent* as their food writer. She has been principal cookery writer on the *Mail on Sunday*'s *YOU Magazine* for over twenty years.

Awarded Journalist of the Year by the Guild of Food Writers, she continues to contribute to a wide variety of national newspapers and magazines, in addition to writing her own titles.

She is author of twenty cookery books.

Annie is married to the landscape architect Jonathan Bell. They have two sons and divide their time between West London and Normandy.

ACKNOWLEDGEMENTS

Eat to Save The Planet was orchestrated by the enthusiasm of publisher Carole Tonkinson. The fact that we can all eat in a way that ensures a greener future for the world embodies the spirit of Pan Macmillan's new imprint One Boat: we are all in this together. So it has been a team effort from the word go.

I want to thank everyone at One Boat, in particular Martha Burley, Managing Editor, for seamlessly steering the project from start to finish, together with Isabel Hewitt, Desk Editor. And thanks to the wider team of Jess Duffy, Sian Gardiner, Jodie Mullish, Brìd Enright, Zainab Dawood, Lindsay Nash and Mel Four, while Jane Bamforth smoothed out the bumps with her meticulous copy-editing.

I am especially grateful to Walter Willett, Professor of Epidemiology and Nutrition at Harvard T.H. Chan School of Public Health, who co-chaired the report 'Food in the Anthropocene', for sharing the background to the report and his vision for putting the science into practice. The other authors of the report whom I want to thank are Dr Marco Springman, Senior Researcher in Population Health at the Oxford Martin School, University of Oxford, for sharing his modelling with me, and Pamela Mason, public health nutritionist with a Master's in Food Policy and specialist interest in sustainable diets, for expanding on the report's content. Also Tim Lang, Professor of Food Policy at the Centre for Food Policy at City University of London, for helping with my research. Thanks also to my niece Lucy Wansbury, and to Dr Jessica Fanzo.

Thanks to my agent Lizzy Kremer at David Higham Associates, for her vision for the book and her support throughout writing it. And to Jonnie, Louis and Rothko, who have been eating the science ever since, and are now experts on whole grains in their rich diversity as well as every other kind of plant food on offer.

INDEX

A

almonds: mint and almond pesto 98
  roast cabbage with almonds 160
amaranth 55, 56, 194
anchovy rainbow chard 172–3
ancient grains 18, 53, 194
animal welfare 20
apples 34, 36
  breakfast pancakes 76
  roast celeriac, carrot and apple 144
  root veg and apple pie 124
asparagus 36
  asparagus speltotto with crab 198
  halloumi pittas with poached eggs 73
  roast beetroot and asparagus roast 142–3
  watercress and asparagus with green pea penne 211
aubergines: aubergine-wrapped Greek sausages 174–5
  chilli beef pie with aubergine 127–8
  vegan burgers 169–70
  vegan chilli 92
avocados: avo nut butter 228
  broad bean guacamole 71
  quinoa and sugar snap stir-fry 176

B

balsamic dressing 135
bananas 32, 38–9
  banana pancakes with maple syrup 46
  berry banana smoothie 44
  breakfast pancakes 76
  exotic smoothie 44–5
barley 50, 51
basa: herby seafood stew 105
basil: basil and pistachio pesto 203–4
  tomato and basil lasagne 118–19
beans: cassoulet with walnut crumbs 122
  garlicky white beans with spinach 110–11
  healthy planet steak and mash 177
  see also individual types of beans
beef: beef hotpot 94
  chilli beef pie with aubergine 127–8
  healthy planet burgers 168
  healthy planet chilli con carne 91
  healthy planet steak and mash 177
beetroot 34, 35, 36
  beetroot mash with wild mushrooms 156
  orange and beetroot salad 180–1
  roast beetroot and asparagus roast 142–3
berries 32
  berry banana smoothie 44
  breakfast pancakes 76
best before dates (BBE) 29–30, 38
Bircher muesli 232
black bean spaghetti: black bean spaghetti with sausage and peppers 210
black beans: herby seafood stew 105
  vegan burgers 169–70
borlotti beans: healthy planet steak and mash 177
born-again bread 43
bran 49, 50
bread 31–2, 194
  born-again bread 43
  halloumi pittas with poached eggs 73
  healthy planet burgers 168
  toasted goat's cheese with garlic spinach 74
  tomato and bread salad 42–3
breakfast 216–17
breakfast pancakes 76
breakfast smoothies 44–5
broad beans 36
  broad bean guacamole 71
  chicken and broad bean stew with pomegranate 95–6
  crispy-topped shepherd's pie 120–1

green vegetable minestrone with mint and almond pesto 98
lamb pilaf with watermelon-and-lemon relish 196–7
minty lamb steaks with anchovy rainbow chard 172–3
broccoli 36
broccoli mash with sesame seeds 158
griddled broccoli and poached eggs with pine nut breadcrumbs 69
Brussels sprouts 34
roast cabbage with almonds 160
buckwheat 18, 55, 56, 86, 194
buckwheat spaghetti, no-cook crab and 209
bulgur wheat 55
aubergine-wrapped Greek sausages with roast tomatoes 174–5
bulgur wheat, cashew nut and rocket pilaf 202
bulgur wheat pilaf 150
lamb pilaf with watermelon-and-lemon relish 196–7
vegan burgers 169–70
burgers: healthy planet burgers 168
vegan burgers 169–70
butter beans: fish pie with pecan crumble 129
healthy planet chilli con carne 91
butternut squash: lamb and butternut stew with pine nuts 100–1

C

cabbage 34
roast cabbage with almonds 160
cacik 197
cannellini beans: cannellini bean mash with roast peppers 155
cannellini bean smash 154
cassoulet with walnut crumbs 122
garlicky white beans with spinach 110–11
capers: tartare sauce 188–9
carbohydrates, complex 47
carrots 34, 35, 36
honey and sesame roast roots 159
Irish stew pie 130–1
roast celeriac, carrot and apple 144
roast chicken and roots with persillade 132
root veg and apple pie 124
cashews: bulgur wheat, cashew nut and rocket pilaf 202
spinach and millet porridge with cashews 200–1
spinach, nut and goat's cheese pie 123
cassoulet with walnut crumbs 122
cauliflower 36
chicken and mushroom pie with cauliflower mash 125–6
ranchos eggs with cauliflower and lentils 68
speedy cauliflower, lentil and watercress risotto 199
spicy cauli with turmeric yoghurt 136
cavolo, crispy salmon with freekeh and 185–6
celeriac: celeriac wedges 162
crispy-topped shepherd's pie 120–1
roast celeriac, carrot and apple 144
straw celeriac cake 163
chard, minty lamb steaks with anchovy rainbow 172–3
cheese 38
cheese oatcakes 233
courgette and goat's cheese with chickpea penne 206
deep-filled mushroom omelette 72
halloumi pittas with poached eggs 73
leek and Emmental scrambled eggs 66
ranchos eggs with cauliflower and lentils 68
spicy Lebanese lamb stew 97
spinach and Parmesan pancakes 78
spinach and scamorza pizza omelette 64–5
spinach, nut and goat's cheese pie 123
supper pancakes 77
toasted goat's cheese with garlic spinach 74
tomato and basil lasagne 118–19
chicken: chicken and broad bean stew with pomegranate 95–6
chicken and mushroom pie with cauliflower mash 125–6

chicken with spinach and padrón peppers 137–8
crispy chicken thighs with fiery chickpea dip 134
paprika chicken with pecan and coriander salsa 171
roast chicken and mushrooms with spelt casarecce 207–8
roast chicken and roots with persillade 132
Thai chicken and edamame bean curry 89–90
tomato and chicken spelt with basil and pistachio pesto 203–4
chickpea penne, courgette and goat's cheese with 206
chickpeas: chilli beef pie with aubergine 127–8
chilli prawn and chickpea stew 102
fiery chickpea dip 134
healthy planet chilli con carne 91
lamb, date and tomato tagine 88
salmon with spinach and chickpeas 190–1
chicory 32
healthy planet steak and mash 177
chillies: chilli beef pie with aubergine 127–8
chilli prawn and chickpea stew 102
coconut dal curry 107–8
healthy planet chilli con carne 91
spicy omelette strips 79–80
Thai chicken and edamame bean curry 89–90
vegan chilli 92–3
chips, courgette 161
cocktail nut pilaf 151
coconut milk: coconut dal curry 107–8
Thai chicken and edamame bean curry 89–90
coffee, freezing 37
condiments 37
confit, red pepper 99
cooking from scratch 28
coriander: pecan and coriander salsa 171
corn 55
corn tortillas with broad bean guacamole and fried eggs 71
courgettes: cassoulet with walnut crumbs 122
courgette and goat's cheese with chickpea penne 206
courgette chips 161
miso-glazed courgette and peppers 145
crab: asparagus speltotto with crab 198
no-cook crab and buckwheat spaghetti 209
cucumber: cacik 197
cucumber and edamame salsa 183–4
herby seafood stew 105
curry 86–7
coconut dal curry 107–8
scallop tikka 106
Thai chicken and edamame bean curry 89–90

D

dairy 17, 38
dal 87
coconut dal curry 107–8
dates: lamb, date and tomato tagine 88
sticky granola balls 234
defrosting food 31
diabetes 15, 21, 53, 148
diets, unhealthy 15, 21
dip, fiery chickpea 134
diseases 15, 21
dressings: balsamic 135
nut butter 235
walnut 182
drinks: smoothies 44–5

E

EAT–*Lancet* Commission 14, 22–3, 148
edamame beans: cucumber and edamame salsa 183–4
miso-glazed courgette and peppers 145
Thai chicken and edamame bean curry 89–90
eggs 20, 38, 59–83
corn tortillas with broad bean guacamole and fried eggs 71
deep-filled mushroom omelette 72
egg-fried spelt 67
fried eggs 82, 83

griddled broccoli and poached eggs with pine nut breadcrumbs 69
halloumi pittas with poached eggs 73
leek and Emmental scrambled eggs 66
pissaladière omelette 62–3
poached eggs 81–2, 83
ranchos eggs with cauliflower and lentils 68
salmon salad niçoise 70
spicy omelette strips 79–80
spinach and scamorza pizza omelette 64–5
toasted goat's cheese with garlic spinach 74
einkorn 51, 53
emmer 51–3
endosperm 49, 50, 53
energy requirements 17, 215
environment, impact on 21–3
exotic smoothie 44–5

F

farro 51–3, 54
faux grains 55–6, 194
fennel 36
fish pie with pecan crumble 129
mackerel with walnut dressing 182
fibre 49, 148
figgy granola 229
fish 17–18, 20, 22, 34
crispy salmon with freekeh and cavolo 185–6
fish pie with pecan crumble 129
frozen fish 39
herby seafood stew 105
mackerel with walnut dressing 182
minty lamb steaks with anchovy rainbow chard 172–3
pan-fried mackerel 108
salmon and spinach with red lentil fusilli 205
salmon salad niçoise 70
salmon with spinach and chickpeas 190–1
seabass fish fingers with tartare sauce 188–9
seared tuna with cucumber and edamame salsa 183–4
sesame mackerel with orange and beetroot salad 180–1
simply salmon and pea fish stew 103
supper pancakes 77
flavour palate 36
flexitarian diets 17, 18–19
'Food in the Anthropocene' report 14, 22
food poverty 15
food production 21–3
freekeh 55, 86
crispy salmon with freekeh and cavolo 185–6
mackerel with walnut dressing 182
pissaladière omelette 62–3
spinach and scamorza pizza omelette 64–5
freezing food 30–1, 37, 39
fridges 30, 219
fruit 29, 34, 36
fruit bowls 38–9
storing 32
see also individual types of fruit
fruit juice: berry banana smoothie 44
exotic smoothie 44–5
frying pans 167

G

garlic 35
garlicky white beans with spinach 110–11
lamb and butternut stew with pine nuts 100–1
spicy Lebanese lamb stew 97
spicy omelette strips 79–80
toasted goat's cheese with garlic spinach 74
germ 49, 50
gherkins: tartare sauce 188–9
ginger: spicy omelette strips 79–80
glycaemic index 53, 149
goat's cheese: courgette and goat's cheese with chickpea penne 206
deep-filled mushroom omelette 72
spinach, nut and goat's cheese pie 123
supper pancakes 77
toasted goat's cheese with garlic spinach 74
grains 34–5

ancient grains 18, 53, 194
cooking 51
faux grains 55
polished grains 50
refined grains 48, 49
whole grains 47–56, 86–7, 166, 194–5, 216
granola: figgy granola 229
sticky granola balls 234
grapes: Bircher muesli 232
green beans: salmon salad niçoise 70
spicy Lebanese lamb stew 97
green pea penne, watercress and asparagus with 211
green vegetable minestrone with mint and almond pesto 98
greenhouse gases 19, 21, 22
guacamole, broad bean 71

H

halloumi pittas with poached eggs 73
haricot beans: cassoulet with walnut crumbs 122
garlicky white beans with spinach 110–11
haricot bean smash 154
hazelnuts: figgy granola 229
healthy planet burgers 168
healthy planet chilli con carne 91–3
healthy planet lasagne 116–17
healthy planet steak and mash 177
herbs 33, 36
herb purée 43–4
herby seafood stew 105
honey: figgy granola 229
honey and sesame roast roots 159
hotpot, beef 94

I

ingredients 219
Irish stew pie 130–1

L

lamb: aubergine-wrapped Greek sausages with roast tomatoes 174–5
crispy-topped shepherd's pie 120–1
healthy planet lasagne 116–17
Irish stew pie 130–1
lamb and butternut stew with pine nuts 100–1
lamb, date and tomato tagine 88
lamb pilaf with watermelon-and-lemon relish 196–7
minty lamb steaks with anchovy rainbow chard 172–3
rack of lamb with pesto potatoes 140–1
spicy Lebanese lamb stew 97
lasagne: healthy planet lasagne 116–17
tomato and basil lasagne 118–19
leaves 36
leeks: asparagus speltotto with crab 198
chicken and broad bean stew with pomegranate 95–6
healthy planet lasagne 116–17
leek and Emmental scrambled eggs 66
legumes 19
lemons: beef hotpot with pickled lemon 94
lemon and pine nut brown rice pilaf 152–3
watermelon-and-lemon relish 196–7
lentil fusilli, salmon and spinach with red 205
lentils 87
healthy planet burgers 168
healthy planet chilli con carne 91
healthy planet lasagne 116–17
ranchos eggs with cauliflower and lentils 68
roast chicken and roots with persillade 132
speedy cauliflower, lentil and watercress risotto 199
vegan chilli 92
lettuce 32, 34, 36
lists, shopping 27
lunch 217

M

mackerel: mackerel with walnut dressing 182
pan-fried mackerel 108
sesame mackerel with orange and beetroot salad 180–1
malnutrition 15, 21
mango: exotic smoothie 44–5
maple syrup, banana pancakes with 46
Marine Stewardship Council (MSC) 20

mayonnaise: mustard mayo 169
tartare sauce 188–9
meal plans 214–27
meat 17–18, 34, 39, 86, 114–15, 166
see also beef; lamb, *etc*
Mediterranean diet 16, 18
milk 38
millet 18, 53, 54, 194
spinach and millet porridge with cashews 200–1
minestrone, green vegetable 98
mint 33
mint and almond pesto 98
mint yoghurt 200–1
minty lamb steaks with anchovy rainbow chard 172–3
pea and mint mash 157
miso-glazed courgette and peppers 145
muesli, Bircher 232
multi-grain porridge 230
mushrooms 34
beetroot mash with wild mushrooms 156
chicken and mushroom pie with cauliflower mash 125–6
deep-filled mushroom omelette 72
healthy planet steak and mash 177
roast chicken and mushrooms with spelt casarecce 207–8
seabass fish fingers 188–9
supper pancakes 77
vegan chilli 92
vegan 'steaks' 178
mustard mayo 169

N

no-cook crab and buckwheat spaghetti 209
nut butter: avo nut butter 228
nut butter dressing 235
nutrition 15, 48
nuts 19, 34–5, 37, 166
cocktail nut pilaf 151
spinach, nut and goat's cheese pie 123
see also individual types of nuts

O

oats 55
Bircher muesli 232
cheese oatcakes 233
figgy granola 229
fish pie with pecan crumble 129
whole oat porridge 230
oils 16, 37
olives: beef hotpot with olives 94
crispy-topped shepherd's pie 120–1
pissaladière omelette 62–3
salmon salad niçoise 70
tomato and bread salad 42–3
omelettes: deep-filled mushroom omelette 72
pissaladière omelette 62–3
spicy omelette strips 79–80
spinach and scamorza pizza omelette 64–5
onions 35
chicken and mushroom pie with cauliflower mash 125–6
orange and beetroot salad 180–1

P

pancakes: banana pancakes with maple syrup 46
breakfast pancakes 76
simply pancakes 75–6
spinach and Parmesan pancakes 78
straw celeriac cake 163
supper pancakes 77
papaya: exotic smoothie 44–5
paprika chicken with pecan and coriander salsa 171
Paris Agreement 15, 23
pasta 54, 194, 195
black bean spaghetti with sausage and peppers 210
courgette and goat's cheese with chickpea penne 206
healthy planet lasagne 116–17
no-cook crab and buckwheat spaghetti 209
roast chicken and mushrooms with spelt casarecce 207–8
salmon and spinach with red lentil fusilli 205
tomato and basil lasagne 118–19
watercress and asparagus with green pea penne 211

peanut butter: avo nut butter 228
pearl barley: Irish stew pie 130–1
pears 34, 36
peas 36
green vegetable minestrone with mint and almond pesto 98
pea and mint mash 157
rack of lamb with pesto potatoes 140–1
scallop tikka 106
simply salmon and pea fish stew 103
pecans: fish pie with pecan crumble 129
nut butter dressing 235
pecan and coriander salsa 171
peppers: black bean spaghetti with sausage and peppers 210
cannellini bean mash with roast peppers 155
chicken with spinach and padrón peppers 137–8
chilli beef pie with aubergine 127–8
healthy planet lasagne 116–17
miso-glazed courgette and peppers 145
paprika chicken with pecan and coriander salsa 171
red pepper confit 99
supper pancakes 77
tomato and chicken spelt with basil and pistachio pesto 203–4
vegan chilli 92
persillade 132
pescatarian diets 18–19
pesto 144
basil and pistachio pesto 203–4
mint and almond pesto 98
pesto potatoes 140–1
pies: chicken and mushroom pie with cauliflower mash 125–6
chilli beef pie with aubergine 127–8
fish pie with pecan crumble 129
Irish stew pie 130–1
root veg and apple pie 124
spinach, nut and goat's cheese pie 123
pilaf 86, 195
bulgur wheat, cashew nut and rocket pilaf 202
bulgur wheat pilaf 150
cocktail nut pilaf 151
lamb pilaf with watermelon-and-lemon relish 196–7
lemon and pine nut brown rice pilaf 152–3
pine nuts: griddled broccoli and poached eggs with pine nut breadcrumbs 69
lamb and butternut stew with pine nuts 100–1
lemon and pine nut brown rice pilaf 152–3
pistachios: basil and pistachio pesto 203–4
Bircher muesli 232
spicy Lebanese lamb stew 97
pitta breads: halloumi pittas with poached eggs 73
pizza-style omelettes: pissaladière omelette 62–3
spinach and scamorza pizza omelette 64–5
Planetary Health Diet 14–15, 23
eggs 60
energy requirements 17, 215
Health Diet Challenge 214–36
how to eat 16–17
potatoes 47, 148
vegans, vegetarians, pescatarians and flexitarians 18–19
waste 25
plant foods 19, 20
pomegranate, chicken and broad bean stew with 95–6
pork: cassoulet with walnut crumbs 122
porridge: multi-grain porridge 230
serving ideas 231
spinach and millet porridge with cashews 200–1
whole oat porridge 230
portion control 25
potatoes 33, 34, 35, 47, 148–9
pea and mint mash 157
rack of lamb with pesto potatoes 140–1
straw celeriac cake 163
poultry 17–18, 20, 34
see also chicken
prawns: chilli prawn and chickpea stew 102
herby seafood stew 105
prepping food 35

processed food 27–8, 35
protein 17–18, 166
animal 19, 86
plant 19
pseudo-grains 55–6, 194
pulses 34–5, 166

Q

quinoa 18, 55, 56, 194
quinoa and sugar snap stir-fry 176

R

radishes 32, 34
rainbow chard, minty lamb steaks with anchovy 172–3
raisins: breakfast pancakes 76
ranchos eggs with cauliflower and lentils 68
raspberries: Bircher muesli 232
relish, watermelon-and-lemon 196–7
rice 50, 53
lemon and pine nut brown rice pilaf 152–3
roast beetroot and asparagus roast 142–3
wild rice 54–5, 194
riches from the rubble soup 40–1
risotto, speedy cauliflower, lentil and watercress 199
rocket: bulgur wheat, cashew nut and rocket pilaf 202
salmon salad niçoise 70
Romanesco: roast Romanesco and spring onion salad with balsamic dressing 135
root vegetables: honey and sesame roast roots 159
roast chicken and roots with persillade 132
root veg and apple pie 124
rye 53

S

salads 32, 34
orange and beetroot salad 180–1
roast Romanesco and spring onion salad 135
salmon salad niçoise 70
tomato and bread salad 42–3
salmon 39
crispy salmon with freekeh and cavolo 185–6
fish pie with pecan crumble 129
salmon and spinach with red lentil fusilli 205
salmon salad niçoise 70
salmon with spinach and chickpeas 190–1
simply salmon and pea fish stew 103
supper pancakes 77
salsa: cucumber and edamame salsa 183–4
pecan and coriander salsa 171
sauces: slow-roasted tomato 104
tartare 188–9
sausages: aubergine-wrapped Greek sausages with roast tomatoes 174–5
black bean spaghetti with sausage and peppers 210
scallop tikka 106
scamorza: spinach and scamorza pizza omelette 64–5
scraps, using 39–46
seabass fish fingers with tartare sauce 188–9
seafood stew, herby 105
seeds, roasted 45
sesame seeds: broccoli mash with sesame seeds 158
honey and sesame roast roots 159
sesame mackerel with orange and beetroot salad 180–1
silken tofu with sesame 236
shepherd's pie, crispy-topped 120–1
shopping 26–7
simply salmon and pea fish stew 103
skins 35
smoked salmon: supper pancakes 77
smoothies 44–5
snacks 217–18
soups: green vegetable minestrone 98
riches from the rubble soup 40–1
soya beans *see* edamame beans
spaghetti: black bean spaghetti with sausage and peppers 210
no-cook crab and buckwheat spaghetti 209
speedy cauliflower, lentil and watercress risotto 199
spelt 18, 50, 51, 53, 54, 86, 194

asparagus speltotto with crab 198
cheese oatcakes 233
egg-fried spelt 67
mackerel with walnut dressing 182
spinach and scamorza pizza omelette 64–5
tomato and chicken spelt with basil and pistachio pesto 203–4
vegan 'steaks' 178
spelt casarecce, roast chicken and mushrooms with 207–8
spelt flour: simply pancakes 75–6
speltotto: asparagus speltotto with crab 198
spices 30, 37
spicy cauli with turmeric yoghurt 136
spicy Lebanese lamb stew 97
spicy omelette strips 79–80
spinach: beef hotpot with olives and pickled lemon 94
chicken with spinach and padrón peppers 137–8
garlicky white beans with spinach 110–11
green vegetable minestrone with mint and almond pesto 98
herby seafood stew 105
lamb, date and tomato tagine 88
pesto 144
salmon and spinach with red lentil fusilli 205
salmon with spinach and chickpeas 190–1
spinach and millet porridge with cashews 200–1
spinach and Parmesan pancakes 78
spinach and scamorza pizza omelette 64–5
spinach, nut and goat's cheese pie 123
toasted goat's cheese with garlic spinach 74
spring onions: courgette and goat's cheese with chickpea penne 206
crispy-topped shepherd's pie 120–1
herby seafood stew 105
roast Romanesco and spring onion salad with balsamic dressing 135
stalks 36
stews 86–7
chicken and broad bean stew with pomegranate 95–6
chilli prawn and chickpea stew 102
herby seafood stew 105
Irish stew pie 130–1
lamb and butternut stew with pine nuts 100–1
lamb, date and tomato tagine 88
simply salmon and pea fish stew 103
spicy Lebanese lamb stew 97
sticky granola balls 234
stir-fry, quinoa and sugar snap 176
stock 32, 35
vegetable stock 41–2
storing food 31–3, 36
straw celeriac cake 163
sugar snaps: quinoa and sugar snap stir-fry 176
sunflower seeds: sticky granola balls 234
supper 217, 219
supper pancakes 77
sweetcorn 34
chilli beef pie with aubergine 127–8

T

tagines 86–7
lamb, date and tomato tagine 88
tartare sauce 188–9
teff 54, 194
Thai chicken and edamame bean curry 89–90
tikka, scallop 106
tofu: silken tofu with sesame 236
Thai tofu and pea curry 90
tofu with chicken and padrón peppers 138
tomatoes 34, 35
aubergine-wrapped Greek sausages with roast tomatoes 174–5
black bean spaghetti with sausage and peppers 210
cassoulet with walnut crumbs 122
chilli beef pie with aubergine 127–8
chilli prawn and chickpea stew 102
crispy-topped shepherd's pie 120–1
fish pie with pecan crumble 129
healthy planet chilli con carne 91
healthy planet lasagne 116–17
lamb and butternut stew with pine nuts 100–1